T0360489

'The idea of a Grounded Economics is an important corrective to economics' long history of excessive abstraction. This book makes a significant contribution to this in its thoughtful analysis of economic agency, and particularly in its argument that agents can transform the worlds they occupy. Strongly recommended – an innovative, original examination of the foundations of economic science.'

John B. Davis, University of Amsterdam and Marquette University

Transformation, Agency and the Economy

Producing, buying, selling, inventing, destroying, caring, imagining, failing – with their everyday practices, people bring about what we call 'the economy'. In order to both understand and transform these practices in the context of mounting socio-ecological challenges, respective knowledge on economic practices becomes crucial. Yet, when it comes to the respective scientific discipline – economics – such knowledge is limited due to a long-standing tradition of favouring abstraction and modelling over assessing real-world economic action. By contrast, this book draws the contours of an economics grounded in real-world phenomena and experiences by outlining the foundations of a Grounded Economics. Building on the philosophical traditions of pragmatism, phenomenology and critical realism, and basic concepts from institutional thought and social scientific practice theories, the book provides a consistent framework to grasp the economy as an 'unfolding process'. By putting forward a strong account of economic agency, the framework allows to identify and differentiate between multiple pathways for social transformations. The book addresses readers from all branches of the social sciences seeking a new vision for economic research, particularly within political economy, heterodox economics, science studies and economic sociology.

Lukas Bäuerle is a post-doctoral researcher at the University of Hamburg. He obtained his doctoral degree at the University of Flensburg with a thesis on a praxeological foundation of economics. His main research interests are institutional economics, social theories of practice as well as economic education and the role of economic knowledge in societal transitions.

Economics and Humanities
Series Editor: Sebastian Berger
University of the West of England (UWE Bristol), UK.

The *Economics and Humanities* series presents the economic wisdom of the humanities and arts. Its volumes gather the economic senses sheltered and revealed by some of the most excellent sources within philosophy, poetry, art, and story-telling. By re-rooting economics in its original domain these contributions allow economic phenomena and their meanings to come into the open more fully; indeed, they allow us to ask anew the question "What is economics?". Economic truth is thus shown to arise from the Human rather than the Market.

Readers will gain a foundational understanding of a humanities-based economics and find their economic sensibility enriched. They should turn to this series if they are interested in questions such as: What are the economic consequences of rooting economic Truth in the Human? What is the purpose of a humanities-based economics? What is the proper meaning of the "oikos", and how does it arise? What are the true meanings of wealth and poverty, gain and loss, capital and productivity? In what sense is economic reasoning with words more fundamental than reasoning with numbers? What is the dimension and measure of human dwelling in the material world?

These volumes address themselves to all those who are interested in sources and foundations for economic wisdom. Students and academics who are fundamentally dissatisfied with the state of economics and worried that its crisis undermines society will find this series of interest.

A New Economic Anthropology
François Régis Mahieu

Transformation, Agency and the Economy
The Case for a Grounded Economics
Lukas Bäuerle

For more information about this series, please visit: www.routledge.com/Economics-and-Humanities/book-series/RSECH

Transformation, Agency and the Economy

The Case for a Grounded Economics

Lukas Bäuerle

Routledge
Taylor & Francis Group

LONDON AND NEW YORK

First published 2023
by Routledge
4 Park Square, Milton Park, Abingdon, Oxon OX14 4RN

and by Routledge
605 Third Avenue, New York, NY 10158

Routledge is an imprint of the Taylor & Francis Group, an informa business

© 2023 Lukas Bäuerle

The right of Lukas Bäuerle to be identified as author of this work has been asserted in accordance with sections 77 and 78 of the Copyright, Designs and Patents Act 1988.

British Library Cataloguing-in-Publication Data
A catalogue record for this book is available from the British Library

ISBN: 978-1-032-44344-7 (hbk)
ISBN: 978-1-032-44345-4 (pbk)
ISBN: 978-1-003-37168-7 (ebk)

DOI: 10.4324/9781003371687

Typeset in Bembo
by Apex CoVantage, LLC

Contents

Foreword   *viii*

1   Introduction   1

2   Lifeworld, sense-making and the primordial gap   11

3   Agents, institutions and the horizontal gap   17

4   Praxis, reflection and the vertical gap   53

5   What is the economy? An interim conclusion   76

6   Grounded economics   85

7   Conclusion   113

Index   *118*

Foreword

The man of System . . . is often so enamoured with the supposed beauty of his own ideal plan of government, that he cannot suffer the smallest deviation from any part of it. He goes on to establish it completely and in all its parts, without any regard either to the great interests, or to the strong prejudices which may oppose it. He seems to imagine that he can arrange the different members of a great society with as much ease as the hand arranges the different pieces upon a chess-board. He does not consider that the pieces upon the chess-board have no other principle of motion besides that which the hand impresses upon them; but that, in the great chess-board of human society, every single piece has a principle of motion of its own, altogether different from that which the legislature might chuse to impress upon it.

Adam Smith

In our vital need – so we are told – this science has nothing to say to us. It excludes in principle precisely the questions which man, given over in our unhappy times to the most portentous upheavals, finds the most burning: questions of the meaning or meaninglessness of the whole of this human existence. Do not these questions, universal and necessary for all men, demand universal reflections and answers based on rational insight? In the final analysis they concern man as a free, self-determining being in his behavior toward the human and extra-human surrounding world and free in regard to his capacities for rationally shaping himself and his surrounding world. What does science have to say about reason and unreason or about us men as subjects of this freedom? The mere science of bodies clearly has nothing to say; it abstracts from everything subjective.

Edmund Husserl

In a nutshell, Smith and Husserl point to the central topics of this book: how can we build a (social) scientific stance that actually grants people the capacities to move on their own – their agency? And what understanding of 'the economy' – reaching out far beyond the black and white of a chess board – arises from there? As Husserl indicates, these questions require us to re-ground the meaning of (economic) science in relation to crisis-laden times at the cost of far-reaching paradigmatic renewal.

1 Introduction

In the context of escalating endeavours to transform the economy towards more sustainable grounds, an old (see Smith) yet simple observation is regaining attention: the economy is made by people. Hence, it can certainly be altered by people into desired directions. So far, so simple? Certainly not! Within the neoliberal imagination, for instance, the economy appears as a result "of human action but not of human design" (Hayek 1967). Yes, the economy may be brought into being by human beings, but it cannot and shall not (!) be designed by them; so runs the general argument. This power is delegated to driving forces behind the scenes, most prominently 'The Market Mechanism' and/or the guardians and proper facilitators of it. For ordinary participants of the economy, there is only agency *within* the Market Order but never beyond or onto the Order itself. The Market Mechanism, formulated by 'Men of System' enjoys a preordained status, miraculously reigning or at least efficiently guiding economic action.

For transformative ambitions, these supposedly scholarly intricacies are of paramount importance. For now, in a historical moment where the calls for radical economic change are mounting, good advice is as scarce as ever. The imaginative and reflexive resources we collectively rely on in economic matters are so thinned out to the margins that it appears to be easier to "imagine the end of the world, rather than the end of capitalism" (Mark Fisher). As the *Social Studies of Economics* (Maeße et al. 2021) insist, economic science itself plays a decisive role when it comes to perpetuating this imaginative deadlock. How so? First, as an abundance of empirical studies have shown, economics is marked by a high degree of internal streamlining or concentration in paradigmatic (Claveau and Gingras 2016; Glötzl and Aigner 2019), institutional (Aistleitner, Kapeller, and Steinerberger 2019; Hodgson and Rothman 1999; Jones and Sloan 2020; Rossier 2020) and social terms (Bayer and Rouse 2016; Chelwa 2021; LeBaron et al. 2021; Lundberg and Stearns 2019), orienting the discipline's development beyond geographical boundaries (Fourcade 2006). In terms of content, or its paradigmatic core, economics has developed on (Claveau and Gingras 2016; Dobusch and Kapeller 2009; Düppe 2009) and

DOI: 10.4324/9781003371687-1

continues to introduce (Bäuerle 2021; Graupe 2012; Hill and Myatt 2010) a picture of 'the economy' as a self-sufficient, harmoniously working 'Market Mechanism', usually depicted on the Circular Flow Diagram (Schlaudt 2022:1.3; Ötsch 2019:4). The arena of economic action is conceived as a self-referential, smoothly functioning sphere in both micro- and macroeconomics. Such a simplistic notion of the economic arena has been continuously criticised from various angles. Most prominently, ecological economists highlighted early on (Daly 1973) that the economy is always embedded in and dependent on nature (Common and Stagl 2005; Raworth 2017). Hence, what is economically feasible or desirable has to be reflected against the ecological fundamentals and boundaries it builds on. Economic sociologists and anthropologists as well as socioeconomists point to the fact that every economic action is embedded in a wider scope of social and cultural institutions that enable 'doing' the economy in the first place (Polanyi 1968; Granovetter 1985). Without institutions, such as language, laws and artifacts, any kind of economic activity, including those running on markets, would be impossible. Since these institutions are not only additive but foundational to the economy, their intellectual neglect is inadequate. Finally, what we call 'the economy' is itself the object of ongoing debates. As feminist economists (Waring 1988; Berik and Kongar 2021), for instance, note, the largely unpaid but absolutely necessary care work, mostly carried out by women, is not accounted for in the standard-economic 'big picture' of the economy, although in many national cases, it surpasses the amount of work (counted in hours) carried out in paid work. Another example of largely neglected economic practices in the discussion of 'the economy' are those in the maintenance of commons (Ostrom 1990; Bollier and Helfrich 2019), where groups or societies manage a joint resource without relying on markets or states, but instead rely on mutual cooperation. Such examples demonstrate that 'the economy' is more diverse than one might assume, based on powerful narratives partly originating from academic economics.

All of these critiques are important in the contemporary assessment of economic discourse. This book will explore and integrate some of them in its ambition to present a new framework of economic reasoning. Nevertheless, specific emphasis is laid on the *capabilities* granted to economic agents by economic science. Normally, these capabilities are reduced to a purely calculative, self-interested and means-to-an-end form of reasoning. Since behavioural economics has ascended to mainstream economics (Frid-Nielsen and Jensen 2020), these 'System 2' capabilities were amended by 'System 1' capabilities (Kahneman 2013): the quasi-automatic reproduction of unconscious patterns of thought and action. As Chapter 4 will demonstrate, this binary set of capabilities falls fatally short of the abundance of human agency, whether conceived for individuals, organisations or entire economies. Crucially, the discipline so far fails to offer agents the attribution of meaning or purpose to their actions, resulting in the implicit reproduction of given ends, the most dominant of which is a single-purpose pecuniary motive, such as income on the micro-level, rents on the meso-level and GDP on the macro-level. In other words, the dominant economics chessboard is populated by a limited set of pawns, the moves of which are restricted to a degree that render 'the human factor' in economic matters barely recognisable and, most importantly, reluctant to far- and deep-reaching transformation.

Now, out of its partial marriage with the political project of neoliberalism (Mirowski and Plehwe 2009; Ötsch, Pühringer, and Hirte 2018), standard-economic imaginaries not only limited the possibilities of thinking about 'the economy' but actually translated into the real-world streamlining of all sorts of social and cultural environments – a development dubbed the 'economisation of the social' (Çalışkan and Callon 2009; Bröckling, Krasmann, and Lemke 2011; Schimank and Volkmann 2012; Wenzlaff 2019). As John B. Davis (2017:525) states, economics since the 1980s "constructs the world in its own image, rather than seeks to provide accurate descriptions of it" (cf. also Mirowski and Nik-Khah 2017:10).[1] Donald MacKenzie and Yuval Millo (2003:108) phrase it: "economics does not describe an existing external 'economy', but brings that economy into being: economics performs the economy, creating the phenomena it describes". As uncounted examples demonstrate, the process of subjecting the world to a specific, utterly limited understanding of 'the economy' has indeed been effective in many cases (cf. Adaman and Madra 2014; Akyel 2013; Mader, Mertens, and Zwan 2020; Spring 2015). If openly imperialistic only in extreme accounts (Becker 1993), economics can rightly be labelled as a 'market-constructivist' (Zuidhof 2014) enterprise. In this vein, being able 'to speak with one voice' has certainly contributed to the discipline's ability to radiate far beyond the academic borders into the social fabric. Taken together, a specific tension arises, marking an all-too-problematic status quo of academic economics as embedded in nature and society: while intellectually abandoning the world[2] (cf. Düppe 2009; Lawson 1997; Pühringer and Bäuerle 2019; Schlaudt 2022:1.3), it has been highly active in it performatively (MacKenzie, Muniesa, and Siu 2007; Cochoy, Giraudeau, and McFall 2010; Boldyrev and Svetlova 2016; Brisset 2018; Maesse 2021).

Whether deliberatively pursued by imperialist ambitions or collaterally supported by institutional default, economists have been heavily involved in developing and disseminating their home-made 'social imaginaries'[3] (Castoriadis 1997), shaping the world according to them, rather than understanding the world and its intricacies in the first place. In constructing the world according to its own image, economics, "the science of managing limited resources, has become an argument for forgetting all limits . . . before finding themselves coping with *finitude* again" (Latour 2020:14). As I will argue, this limitlessness of economics is rooted in its refusal to accept the tangible world as ineluctable ground, as friction, as an epistemic partner to be coped with. Rather, the world appears as the infinite appliance field for infinitely applicable concepts which do not gain their legitimacy out of a sound resemblance of (aspects of) the world but out of the power to inspire social change towards a non-disputed imagination (Harcourt 2012; Ötsch 2019; Zuidhof 2012). That is to say, in spite of informing transformative agents on possible next moves, economics is itself deeply entrenched in problematic imaginaries that have made radical transformation necessary in the first place. And, through its institutionalised impact on societies around the globe, the discipline's ongoing inability to innovate on paradigmatic levels affects us all and our prospects for collective renewal. From a discrepancy between the need and will to 'do' the economy differently, on the one hand, and the intellectual resources informing such action, on the other, arises a stark field of tension. Certainly, scientific discourses may only represent one resource on this field – but they are an important and, in many national cases, a publicly funded one.

Against this background, the present book sets out to imagine a new relationship between economics and the lifeworld – a relationship built from the primacy and ineluctability of the latter, rather than the former. To this end, a new understanding of 'the economy' as a collective process of sense-making embedded in and referring to the lifeworld will be developed both verbally and graphically in the form of a concise framework. In doing so, the book will come across questions such as: What real-world economies would actually come into the scientific gaze if we freed this very gaze from its imaginary ballast? How could a different econo-scientific gaze be constructed, keen to understand how people actually 'do' the economy 'out there'? What kinds of transformative potentials would come into sight if 'the economy' would not be confounded with 'economic theory' but were seen as an emergent social process of doing, saying, thinking things in its name? How can we distinguish between different forms of economic action and in what way do they affect people's agency – the capability of moving beyond the collectively taken-for-granted? If economic reasoning is tied to its wider socio-cultural context, what would a form of economic reasoning look like that tries to put the phenomenon of economic agency centre stage without streamlining it towards a science-induced direction? How could economics become a co-creative partner rather than a director of the social processes it engages with? How could it raise the reflexive intensity of this process by reconstructing its central architecture as well as its potentials? The tentative answers to these questions will lead us to a 'Grounded Economics' in a double sense: (1) a science advancing in the consciousness of its own ever-embeddedness in socio-ecological contexts and (2) a science securing a sound relationship to the phenomena it is coping with in epistemic terms.

Before we set out to explore Grounded Economics and its underlying framework, two fundamental assertions shall be singled out which build a kind of intellectual undercurrent for the entire argument and also led to the title of the book. First and foremost, 'economic transformation' is not a contemporary imperative but a precise description of how 'the economy' has always been evolving in time and space. A first step towards transformation would be to conceive the economy as 'an unfolding process' (Veblen 1898:388) that, as of today, is unfolding as a 'racing standstill': an escalating, performative reproduction of ever-sameness. Unlearning the dead imaginaries of a fixed, 'extra-terrestrial' (Latour 2018) economy as originating partly from academic economics is a crucial step in transformative endeavours. Second, the reason for the economy's ever-transformative character lies in its human origin. For 'the economy' is nothing other than an expression of how people relate to the world, and this relationship is ever-evolving. Hence, remembering the ever-transforming economy is the same as remembering economic agency: action based on potentiality rather than memory (Archer 2000; Unger 2007; Claassen and Herzog 2021). What arises from there is an economic thinking that highlights potentials rather than limitations, aware of ambiguities and disruptions in the everyday making of 'the economy'.

This book aims at filling these voids by providing a comprehensive framework gained from an interplay of social-scientific traditions, having, in large part, resisted the temptations of a growing intellectual dissociation from real-world economic processes. Socioeconomics, and institutionalism alongside it, is certainly one of these fields, having secured ambiguity and critical evolution through interdisciplinary provocations alone. As we shall see, to them, just as to us, philosophical traditions such as pragmatism and social phenomenology have and continue to provide a strong orientation in this vein. At its core, the proposed framework consists of three fundamental fields of tension that are present in any economic situation but, at the same time, fundamentally differ between any two situations. Hence, while the framework allows one to think about 'the economy' anew, it does not anticipate how it presents itself in any particular situation. This always remains an open task for strong, empirical research and cannot (and shall not) be deducted from this or any other conceptual framework.

The book principally resembles a comprehensive introduction of the framework. In order to do so, the work is structured around three fundamental questions: Chapter 2 covers the question of *where* the economy actually takes place. With reference to social phenomenology, it will outline a fundamentally embedded account of the economy as a collective sense-making procedure in reference to an ineluctable lifeworld. Chapter 3 will ask *who* actually does the economy? By critically assessing individualistic and structuralist accounts, it will bring forth first transformative potentials in the ambiguous interplay of agents and social structures. When starting from the fact that 'the economy is made by people', an interesting (and much contested) question arises about *how* this action actually proceeds. Chapter 4 will try to uncover the *modus operandi* of economic action, identifying different forms of practice, all of which bring along their own frictions and potentials for economic transformation. After having answered the question 'What is the economy?' when conceived from the angle of the proposed framework (Chapter 5), a methodological chapter will outline the basic tenets of an economics suitable to approach this economy: the case of a Grounded Economics (Chapter 6). The book concludes with final remarks referring to the transformational endeavours as manifest in recent public discourse and possible contributions of Grounded Economics (Chapter 7). In other words, this book will turn conventional economic pedagogy upside down: instead of inviting you "to set aside that everyday understanding and think of the term or concept as economists do" (Mankiw and Taylor 2014:17), we will start by setting aside the terms and conceptions of mainstream economists and rebuild them to actually enable an open engagement with the everyday world, and more precisely, with the economy as an ever-unfolding process. If economics is yet to advance into a "volitional science, a science of the 'human will in action' [cf. Commons 1934a, 100]" (Albert and Ramstad 1997:885) it will need to drastically innovate its conceptual and methodological inventory: "For change to be meaningful, something meaningful has to change in the way we approach the world" (Banerjee, Carney, and Hulgård 2019:2).

Notes

1 For an early exponent of this specific relationship towards the lifeworld see Walras (1965:71; my emphasis):

> This much is certain, however, that the physico-mathematical sciences . . . do go beyond experience as soon as they have drawn their type concepts from it. From real-type concepts, these sciences abstract ideal-type concepts, which they define, and then, on the basis of these definitions, construct *a priori* the whole framework of their theorems and proofs. After that, they go back to experience *not to confirm but to apply* their conclusions. . . . The return to reality should not take place until the science is completed and then only with a view to practical applications.

2 Along with the so called 'empirical turn' (Angrist et al. 2017; Backhouse and Cherrier 2017; Einav and Levin 2014:716), there seems to settle in a reconnection with Planet Earth in academic economics. Interestingly enough, 'agent-based' or 'experimental' approaches appear to yet again introduce the human factor into economic reasoning along with it. At second sight, this development and its methodological manifestations do provoke a series of question marks. For, in the methodological advances most commonly (cf. Hamermesh 2013:168) running under the 'empirical turn', the capabilities and respective freedoms of agents doing the economy resume to be highly limited; mostly, due to the economists will to end up with definite results by the theoretical ballast carried in the empirical methods at hand. For instance, 'empirical' is all too fast and often being equalised with (numeric) 'data'; whereas the question of data production and the relationship of data to practices of real-world agents *before* the data, just as in other (social) sciences, typically (Greiffenhagen, Mair, and Sharrock 2011) remains an untouched black box (Mügge and Linsi 2020). Against the backdrop of our initial question 'how to transform the economy?', such seemingly far-fetched methodological issues are all-decisive, since every single one of these choices predetermines (and most of the times *limits*) the potentials for economic transformation:

> the quality of ubiquitous economic data is much worse than their users typically acknowledge. . . . If economic data fail to capture what they purportedly claim to represent, public deliberation, economic policy, and academic analysis drawing on them all suffer.
>
> (Mügge and Linsi 2020:2)

In short, even the 'empirical' advances of the discipline have to be assessed with care and case-related precision; are we witnessing a recalibration with tangible phenomena or just a pluralising of methodical mirrors in which economists appear to see themselves, yet again?

3 One could also speak of 'pseudo-environments' (Lippmann 1997), 'cultural frames' (Beckert 2016:88), 'collective tacit knowledge' (Collins 2013:2) or 'paradigms' (Kuhn 1996).

References

Adaman, Fikret, and Yahya M. Madra. 2014. 'Understanding Neoliberalism as Economization: The Case of the Environment'. Pp. 29–51 in Global Economic Crisis and the Politics of Diversity, edited by Y. Atasoy. London: Palgrave Macmillan UK.

Aistleitner, Matthias, Jakob Kapeller, and Stefan Steinerberger. 2019. 'Citation Patterns in Economics and Beyond'. Science in Context 32(4):361–80. https://doi.org/10.1017/S0269889720000022.

Akyel, Dominic. 2013. Die Ökonomisierung der Pietät: der Wandel des Bestattungsmarkts in Deutschland. Frankfurt am Main: Campus Verlag.

Albert, Alexa, and Yngve Ramstad. 1997. 'The Social Psychological Underpinnings of Commons's Institutional Economics: The Significance of Dewey's Human Nature and Conduct'. Journal of Economic Issues 31(4):881–916. https://doi.org/10.1080/002 13624.1997.11505983.

Angrist, Joshua, Pierre Azoulay, Glenn Ellison, Ryan Hill, and Susan Feng Lu. 2017. 'Economic Research Evolves: Fields and Styles'. American Economic Review 107(5):293–97. https://doi.org/10.1257/aer.p20171117.

Archer, Margaret S. 2000. Being Human: The Problem of Agency. Cambridge: Cambridge University Press.

Backhouse, Roger E., and Béatrice Cherrier. 2017. 'The Age of the Applied Economist'. History of Political Economy 49(Supplement):1–33. https://doi.org/10.1215/00182702-4166239.

Banerjee, Swati, Stephen Carney, and Lars Hulgård, eds. 2019. People Centered Social Innovation: Global Perspectives on an Emerging Paradigm. London; New York: Routledge.

Bäuerle, Lukas. 2021. 'The Power of Economics Textbooks. Shaping Meaning and Identity'. in Power and Influence of Economists: Contributions to the Social Studies of Economics, edited by J. Maesse, S. Pühringer, T. Rossier, and P. Benz. London; New York: Routledge.

Bayer, Amanda, and Cecilia Elena Rouse. 2016. 'Diversity in the Economics Profession: A New Attack on an Old Problem'. Journal of Economic Perspectives 30(4):221–42. https://doi.org/10.1257/jep.30.4.221.

Becker, Gary S. 1993. 'Economic Imperialism'. Religion & Liberty 3(2).

Beckert, Jens. 2016. Imagined Futures: Fictional Expectations and Capitalist Dynamics. Cambridge, MA: Harvard University Press.

Berik, Günseli, and Ebru Kongar, eds. 2021. The Routledge Handbook of Feminist Economics. Abingdon, Oxon ; New York, NY: Routledge.

Boldyrev, Ivan, and Ekaterina Svetlova, eds. 2016. Enacting Dismal Science: New Perspectives on the Performativity of Economics. New York: Palgrave Macmillan.

Bollier, David, and Silke Helfrich. 2019. Free, Fair and Alive: The Insurgent Power of the Commons. Gabriola Island: New Society Publishers.

Brisset, Nicolas. 2018. *Economics and Performativity: Exploring Limits, Theories and Cases.* Abingdon, Oxon ; New York, NY: Routledge, 2018. | Series: Routledge INEM advances in economic methodology ; 18: Routledge.

Bröckling, Ulrich, Susanne Krasmann, and Thomas Lemke, eds. 2011. *Governmentality: Current Issues and Future Challenges.* New York: Routledge.

Çalışkan, Koray, and Michel Callon. 2009. 'Economization, Part 1: Shifting Attention from the Economy Towards Processes of Economization'. *Economy and Society* 38(3):369–98. https://doi.org/10.1080/03085140903020580.

Castoriadis, Cornelius. 1997. *The Imaginary Institution of Society.* Cambridge: Polity Press.

Chelwa, Grieve. 2021. 'Does Economics Have an "Africa Problem"?'. *Economy and Society* 50(1):78–99. https://doi.org/10.1080/03085147.2021.1841933.

Claassen, Rutger, and Lisa Herzog. 2021. 'Why Economic Agency Matters: An Account of Structural Domination in the Economic Realm'. *European Journal of Political Theory* 20(3):465–85. https://doi.org/10.1177/1474885119832181.

Claveau, François, and Yves Gingras. 2016. 'Macrodynamics of Economics: A Bibliometric History'. *History of Political Economy* 48(4):551–92. https://doi.org/10.1215/00182702-3687259.

Cochoy, Franck, Martin Giraudeau, and Liz McFall. 2010. 'Performativity, Economics and Politics: An Overview'. *Journal of Cultural Economy* 3(2):139–46. https://doi.org/10.1080/17530350.2010.494116.

Collins, Harry. 2013. *Tacit and Explicit Knowledge.* Chicago, IL: University of Chicago Press.

Common, Michael S., and Sigrid Stagl. 2005. *Ecological Economics: An Introduction.* Cambridge; New York: Cambridge University Press.

Daly, Herman E. 1973. *Toward a Steady-State Economy.* San Francisco: W. H. Freeman.

Davis, John B. 2017. 'Is Mainstream Economics a Science Bubble?'. *Review of Political Economy* 29(4):523–38. https://doi.org/10.1080/09538259.2017.1388983.

Dobusch, Leonhard, and Jakob Kapeller. 2009. '"Why Is Economics Not an Evolutionary Science?" New Answers to Veblen's Old Question'. *Journal of Economic Issues* 43(4):867–98.

Düppe, Till. 2009. 'The Phenomenology of Economics: Life-World, Formalism, and the Invisible Hand'. *Journal of the History of Economic Thought* 32(4):609–6011.

Einav, Liran, and Jonathan Levin. 2014. 'The Data Revolution and Economic Analysis'. *Innovation Policy and the Economy* 14:1–24. https://doi.org/10.1086/674019.

Fourcade, Marion. 2006. 'The Construction of a Global Profession: The Transnationalization of Economics'. *American Journal of Sociology* 112(1):145–94. https://doi.org/10.1086/502693.

Frid-Nielsen, Snorre Sylvester, and Mads Dagnis Jensen. 2020. 'Maps of Behavioural Economics: Evidence from the Field'. *Journal of Interdisciplinary Economics* 33(2):1–25. https://doi.org/10.1177/0260107920925675.

Glötzl, Florentin, and Ernest Aigner. 2019. 'Six Dimensions of Concentration in Economics: Evidence from a Large-Scale Data Set'. *Science in Context* 32(4):381–410. https://doi.org/10.1017/S0269889720000034.

Granovetter, Mark. 1985. 'Economic Action and Social Structure: The Problem of Embeddedness'. *American Journal of Sociology* 91(3):481–510. https://doi.org/10.1086/228311.

Graupe, Silja. 2012. 'The Power of Ideas: The Teaching of Economics and Its Image of Man'. *Journal of Social Science Education* 11(2):60–85. https://doi.org/10.4119/jsse-595.

Greiffenhagen, Christian, Michael Mair, and Wes Sharrock. 2011. 'From Methodology to Methodography: A Study of Qualitative and Quantitative Reasoning in Practice'. *Methodological Innovations Online* 6(3):93–107. https://doi.org/10.4256/mio.2011.009.

Hamermesh, Daniel S. 2013. 'Six Decades of Top Economics Publishing: Who and How?'. *Journal of Economic Literature* 51(1):162–72. https://doi.org/10.1257/jel.51.1.162.

Harcourt, Bernard E. 2012. *The Illusion of Free Markets: Punishment and the Myth of Natural Order*. Cambridge, MA: Harvard University Press.

Hayek, Friedrich. 1967. 'The Results of Human Action but Not of Human Design'. Pp. 96–105 in *Studies in Philosophy, Politics and Economics*. Chicago: University of Chicago Press.

Hill, Rod, and Anthony Myatt. 2010. *The Economics Anti-Textbook: A Critical Thinker's Guide to Microeconomics*. Halifax: Fernwood Publ.

Hodgson, Geoffrey M., and Harry Rothman. 1999. 'The Editors and Authors of Economics Journals: A Case of Institutional Oligopoly?'. *The Economic Journal* 109(453):165–86. https://doi.org/10.1111/1468-0297.00407.

Jones, Todd R., and Arielle Sloan. 2020. 'Staying at the Top: The Ph.D. Origins of Economics Faculty'. *EdWorkingPaper* 20(324).

Kahneman, Daniel. 2013. *Thinking, Fast and Slow*. New York: Farrar, Straus and Giroux.

Kuhn, Thomas S. 1996. *The Structure of Scientific Revolutions*. 3rd ed. Chicago: University of Chicago Press.

Latour, Bruno. 2018. *Down to Earth: Politics in the New Climatic Regime*. Cambridge: Polity Press.

Latour, Bruno. 2020. 'Seven Objections against Landing on Earth'. Pp. 10–19 in *Critical Zones: Observatories for Earthly Politics*, edited by B. Latour and P. Weibel. Cambridge: The MIT Press.

Lawson, Tony. 1997. *Economics and Reality*. London; New York: Routledge.

LeBaron, Genevieve, Daniel Mügge, Jacqueline Best, and Colin Hay. 2021. 'Blind Spots in IPE: Marginalized Perspectives and Neglected Trends in Contemporary Capitalism'. *Review of International Political Economy* 28(2):283–94. https://doi.org/10.1080/09692290.2020.1830835.

Lippmann, Walter. 1997. *Public Opinion*. New Brunswick: Transaction Publishers.

Lundberg, Shelly, and Jenna Stearns. 2019. 'Women in Economics: Stalled Progress'. *Journal of Economic Perspectives* 33(1):3–22. https://doi.org/10.1257/jep.33.1.3.

MacKenzie, Donald A., and Yuval Millo. 2003. 'Constructing a Market, Performing Theory: The Historical Sociology of a Financial Derivatives Exchange'. *American Journal of Sociology* 109(1):107–45. https://doi.org/10.1086/374404.

MacKenzie, Donald A., Fabian Muniesa, and Lucia Siu, eds. 2007. *Do Economists Make Markets?: On the Performativity of Economics*. Princeton: Princeton University Press.

Mader, Philip, Daniel Mertens, and Natascha van der Zwan, eds. 2020. *The Routledge International Handbook of Financialization*. London; New York: Routledge.

Maesse, Jens. 2021. 'Performative, Imaginary and Symbolic Power'. Pp. 19–35 in *Power and Influence of Economists*. London: Routledge.

Maeße, Jens, Stephan Pühringer, Thierry Rossier, and Pierre Benz, eds. 2021. *Power and Influence of Economists: Contributions to the Social Studies of Economics*. London; New York: Routledge.

Mankiw, Gregory, and Mark P. Taylor. 2014. *Economics*. 3rd ed. Andover: Cengage Learning.

10 *Introduction*

Mirowski, Philip, and Edward M. Nik-Khah. 2017. *The Knowledge We Have Lost in Information: The History of Information in Modern Economics.* New York City: Oxford University Press.

Mirowski, Philip, and Dieter Plehwe. 2009. *The Road from Mont Pèlerin: The Making of the Neoliberal Thought Collective.* Cambridge, MA: Harvard University Press.

Mügge, Daniel, and Lukas Linsi. 2020. 'The National Accounting Paradox: How Statistical Norms Corrode International Economic Data'. *European Journal of International Relations* 135406612093633. https://doi.org/10.1177/1354066120936339.

Ostrom, Elinor. 1990. *Governing the Commons: The Evolution of Institutions for Collective Action.* Cambridge; New York: Cambridge University Press.

Ötsch, Walter Otto. 2019. *Mythos Markt. Mythos Neoklassik: das Elend des Marktfundamentalismus.* Marburg: Metropolis.

Ötsch, Walter Otto, Stephan Pühringer, and Katrin Hirte. 2018. *Netzwerke Des Marktes: Ordoliberalismus Als Politische Ökonomie.* Wiesbaden: Springer VS.

Polanyi, Karl. 1968. 'The Economy as Instituted Process'. Pp. 122–42 in *Economic Anthropology: Readings in Theory and Analysis,* edited by E. E. LeClair and H. K. Schneider. New York: Holt, Rinehart, Winston.

Pühringer, Stephan, and Lukas Bäuerle. 2019. 'What Economics Education Is Missing: The Real World'. *International Journal of Social Economics* 46(8):977–91. https://doi.org/10.1108/IJSE-04-2018-0221.

Raworth, Kate. 2017. *Doughnut Economics: Seven Ways to Think Like a 21st-Century Economist.* London: Random House Business Books.

Rossier, Thierry. 2020. 'Accumulation and Conversion of Capitals in Professorial Careers. The Importance of Scientific Reputation, Network Relations, and Internationality in Economics and Business Studies'. *Higher Education* 1061–80. doi:10.1007/s10734-020-00508-3.

Schimank, Uwe, and Ute Volkmann, eds. 2012. *The Marketization of Society: Economizing the Non-Economic.* Bremen: University of Bremen.

Schlaudt, Oliver. 2022. *Philosophy of Economics: A Heterodox Introduction.* Abingdon, Oxon; New York, NY: Routledge.

Spring, Joel H. 2015. *Economization of Education: Human Capital, Global Corporations, Skills-Based Schooling.* New York: Routledge.

Unger, Roberto Mangabeira. 2007. *The Self Awakened: Pragmatism Unbound.* Cambridge, MA: Harvard University Press.

Veblen, Thorstein. 1898. 'Why Is Economics Not an Evolutionary Science?' *The Quarterly Journal of Economics* 12(4):373–97. doi: 10.2307/1882952.

Walras, Léon. 1965. *Elements of Pure Economics.* 2nd ed. Homewood: Richard D. Irwin, Inc.

Waring, Marilyn. 1988. *If Women Counted: A New Feminist Economics.* San Francisco: Harper & Row.

Wenzlaff, Ferdinand. 2019. 'Economization of Society: Functional Differentiation and Economic Stagnation'. *Journal of Economic Issues* 53(1):57–80. https://doi.org/10.1080/00213624.2019.1557001.

Zuidhof, Peter-Wim. 2012. *Imagining Markets: The Discursive Politics of Neoliberalism.* Rotterdam: Erasmus University Rotterdam.

Zuidhof, Peter-Wim. 2014. 'Thinking Like an Economist: The Neoliberal Politics of the Economics Textbook'. *Review of Social Economy* 72(2):157–85. https://doi.org/10.1080/00346764.2013.872952.

2 Lifeworld, sense-making and the primordial gap

The first and central concept of the proposed framework is that of the lifeworld. With reference to the phenomenological tradition, the lifeworld is understood here as a realm that is at once transcendental, tangible and socially shared. The lifeworld is that which raises all lived experiences; it is the 'wherein' of the experiences we make as living human beings:

> The lifeworld is . . . for us, those who live awake in it, always already there, existing for us in advance, 'ground' for all practice, whether theoretical or extra-theoretical. The world is given to us, the awake, the always some-how practically interested subjects, not occasionally once, but always and necessarily given as the universal field of all real and possible practice, as a horizon. Life is living in constant world-certainty.
>
> (Hua VI, 145)[1]

The life-world as just described is a transcendental notion. Rather than an object of intellectual life, the life-world 'constitutes' intellectual life. Husserl put the entrance door to all transcendental phenomenology in the short words: 'The world . . . does not exist as an entity, as an object, but exists with such uniqueness that the plural makes no sense when applied to it' (Hua VI, 146, E.: 144).

> (Düppe 2009:25; with reference to the singularity of
> the lifeworld, see Unger and Smolin 2015)

Our performative, intellectual, discursive, affective, spiritual or other impulses are always already related to a world that we find without demanding it. This world is given, not willed (cf. Merleau-Ponty 2002:385). In this sense, human impulses are late and existentially subordinate. Living human beings always and inevitably establish a relationship towards the lifeworld, whether in the form of wandering through a landscape, buying something in a shop or in the form of negating this relationship. Strictly speaking, the concept of the lifeworld is not a concept that can be 'reached' or 'uncovered' with the help of scientific procedures, for instance. Nor is it an object that can be completely outlined or

DOI: 10.4324/9781003371687-2

mapped. As Husserl states, "The lifeworld is a realm of primordial evidences" (Hua VI, 130). Because of its original or primordial,[2] hence primary, character, it is in principle unreachable.[3] It is that which raises the motivation to reach out in the first place. It is an "inexhaustible supply of otherness, and . . . an irreducible challenge to every established signification" (Castoriadis 1997:371).

The lifeworld, to be clear, is not to be reduced to 'nature', but in another term, perhaps to be grasped as a 'socio-ecological space of experience' – a phenomenal stage on which we always already stand without wanting to.

In a second step, the concept of *sense-making*[4] will now be introduced for the fundamental and everyday *human reference* to the lifeworld following Svetlova:

> Meaning arises from the fact that the subject repeatedly takes a position in relation to the world in a situation. What remains decisive is the process character of the procedure of sense-making: meaning is not predetermined in things, texts or situations. It emerges in the designing and interpreting of actions. . . . When something unfamiliar, i.e., also unexpected, happens, new interpretations are required that make the unusual event appear again as comprehensible in a new context. To enable this classification is the central task of sense-making: a new meaning must be given to the surprising event.
>
> (Svetlova 2008:31; this and all following translations
> of Sveltova 2008 are mine)

Svetlova suggests that the world can never be conclusively interpreted or caught up with. Its primacy entangles the human being in an endless interplay of experiences that repeatedly stimulate us to actualise the meaning of our relationships to the lifeworld but without ever arriving at a completed relationship to it. Out of this process emerge 'social imaginaries': "the creation of significations and the creation of the images and figures that support these significations" (Castoriadis 1997:238). The difference between the experienced lifeworld on the one hand (turquoise background) and socially shared references to it on the other (red areas) is what I call the *primordial gap* (see Figure 2.1). The processes of sense-making can, graphically speaking, never catch up with or cover an imagined totality of the lifeworld. The circle is always larger than the rhombus; the difference is the primordial gap.

Out of the gap emerges a dynamic process of human sense-making that never finds equilibrium or a point of rest. This dynamic is further enhanced by the fact that human references to the lifeworld themselves become part of it. The realisation of significations in the form of lived praxis becomes *in actu*, itself a life-worldly datum (cf. Schütz 1996:27). The lifeworld and the human interpretation of it are, thus, inseparably intertwined (cf. Castoriadis 1997:338–39). As the two following sections will show, the processes of human sense-making are expanded and, as it were, dynamised by two further fields of tension: the tensions between individuality and sociality, on the one hand, and

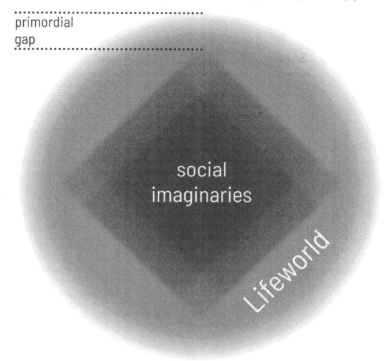

Figure 2.1 Social imaginaries in relation to an unavoidable lifeworld

between praxis and reflection, on the other. All three fields of tension render a conclusive 'mapping', 'solution' or 'deciphering' of an imagined life-worldly entirety and of social reality along with it impossible.

On the other hand, this does not mean that a scientific examination of the lifeworld and human references to it are impossible, for its inexhaustibility, which is also reflected in the metaphors of the lifeworld as *horizon* (Husserl) or *cosmos* (Eugen Fink), is contrasted by its phenomenal appearance in concrete situations. Situations have a place and a time. They consist of observable phenomena, a materiality and corporeality: they are 'matters of concern' (Latour 2005:14). A situation in Madagascar will always differ in many aspects from a situation in Sicily. In these situations, the lifeworld 'shows itself' in the form of phenomena that are accessible to the human experience. Husserl speaks of a 'mode of givenness' of the lifeworld that will still be reflected in the subjectively turned cipher of the 'thrownness of man' (*Geworfenheit des Menschen*) of his student, Heidegger; "the real, bodily man, standing on the solid well-rounded earth, breathing out and breathing in all natural forces" (MEW 40, 577), as Marx called him/her.

Your present situation as a reader, for example, includes at least yourself and this book in analogue or digital form. But it also includes your spatio-temporal situation (i.e., where and when you are reading), the social context (for instance in the form of self-study or a seminar), your emotional state and the surrounding atmosphere (of security, threat, tension), etc. These are some of the elements of the situation you are living through right now and which you are (re)producing in parts through the practice of your reading. With respect to 'the economy', it also always takes place in concrete places and at concrete times (see below) – e.g., during the early shift in the production hall, the harvest season in the fields, 24/7 in front of a screen, a lifetime in the cobalt mine. These are life-worldly situations, where 'the economy' takes place in time.

In addition to the situations, the routinised procedures of coping with them – i.e., in the form of patterns of interpretation, language, decision-making routines, handles, sequences of movements, facial expressions, etc. – are not only tangible and concrete but also always specific. The established routines of sense-making that people bring to a situation stem from social imaginaries that people of a certain tradition, culture or milieu often use without question when encountering the lifeworld. Later, I will introduce the concept of institutions for dealing with them conceptually. Situations and the institutional arrangements found in them give an experience a *specific*, and thus limited, form. Making experiences always means making them *there* and *then* as *this* or *that person* and in *this* or *that way*. Both the specific mode of sense-making and the specific object or 'phenomenal partner' of an experience are thus limited or preconfigured, never 'whole'. They are negotiated and determined in a living interplay between humans and the world in a spatio-temporal situation:

> The creation of instituting society, as instituted society, is each time a common world – *kosmos koinos*: the positing of individuals, of their types, relations and activities; but also the positing of things, their types, relations and signification – all of which are caught up each time in receptacles and frames of reference instituted as common, which make them exist together.
> (Castoriadis 1997:370)

The difference between a situation in Madagascar, on the one hand, and in Sicily, on the other, is thus not only given by the situation (by the phenomenal appearance of the lifeworld) but also by the meaning we attach to the situation as biographical individuals, as members of a group, a language family, etc. (Dolfsma and Verburg 2008:1039–40; cf. Lawson 1987:961–62).

The institutions of sense-making shared by groups or milieus also address their specific mode: sense-making is always a *social reference to the lifeworld*. In a strict sense, one is never alone in a situation; even hermits cultivate discursive and performative references to the lifeworld, which they have learned in a group – i.e., a family. The self-conversation and other practises of self-reference bear witness to this 'social thrownness'. As we will see, social situatedness is by no means to be confused with social determination; it "is undetermined but not unstructured" (Beckert 2003:771). People are always capable of changing what they have learned and normalised socially. However, the default position of human references to the lifeworld is a socially shaped and learned one. This applies to the biographies of individual agents as well as to new social phenomena. They inevitably emerge from 'old' phenomena or 'structures'; from a network of established social imaginaries. And even the most radical, new creation of an ingenious individual is only realised – and becomes meaningful – when placed in established relations. Social realities thus always have a history and always become history (cf. Svetlova 2008:160).

What may initially sound far from standard economic theory is certainly not far off from economic reality. If economic activity does not take place according to quasi-natural laws, but rather, in human sense-making procedures as references to lifeworldly situations, then the stance of Alfred Schütz also applies here: "any science dealing with human affairs and eager to grasp human reality has to be founded on the interpretation of the *lifeworld* by human beings living within it" (Schütz 1996:72). As Chapter 5 will explore in detail, 'the economy' is nothing more (and nothing less!) than what is connected to the term in collective processes of sense-making, be it wider imaginary landscapes and significations or actual people, their practices and material manifestations. Such an understanding of economic processes bears serious consequences for the scientific discussion of the same, not least due to the fundamental ambiguity, contradictoriness and unpredictability of economic practice. Yet there exist numerous pioneers of an economics actually trying to approach 'the economy' as social processes of sense-making in relation to the tangible lifeworld.

Notes

1 If not indicated otherwise, all quotations from Husserl refer to the edition of his works *Husserliana* (Hua) in German, published by Martinus Nijhoff in The Hague and were translated by myself (1954, 1960, 1973).

2 From Latin *primus* (first) and *ordior* (beginning), cf. Lee (2002).

3 This also means that strictly idealistic positions, such as those represented by radical constructivism, which ultimately lead to a dissolution between *epistemata* and *ontos* (and thus also epistemology and ontology), are to be rejected. There is an experiential lifeworld before human reference to it, even if it remains open here whether and to what extent it is possible for individuals to break through this referencing. Rosa discusses respective attempts on 'vertical axes of Resonance' (Rosa 2019: chapter VIII).

4 In the later sections, the concept of sense-making is occasionally used synonymously with the term 'interpretation', which is more common in the social sciences. In the preliminary remarks on the theory of science, the term sense-making is preferred because it emphasises the active and sometimes creative side of interpretive processes.

References

Beckert, Jens. 2003. 'Economic Sociology and Embeddedness: How Shall We Conceptualize Economic Action?'. *Journal of Economic Issues* 37(3):769–87. https://doi.org/1 0.1080/00213624.2003.11506613.

Castoriadis, Cornelius. 1997. *The Imaginary Institution of Society*. Cambridge: Polity Press.

Dolfsma, Wilfred, and Rudi Verburg. 2008. 'Structure, Agency and the Role of Values in Processes of Institutional Change'. *Journal of Economic Issues* 42(4):1031–54. https:// doi.org/10.1080/00213624.2008.11507201.

Düppe, Till. 2009. 'The Phenomenology of Economics: Life-World, Formalism, and the Invisible Hand'. *Journal of the History of Economic Thought* 32(4):609–611.

Husserl, Edmund. 1954. *Die Krisis Der Europäischen Wissenschaften Und Die Transzendentale Phänomenologie: Eine Einleitung in Die Phänomenologische Philosophie*. Den Haag: Martinus Nijhoff.

Husserl, Edmund. 1960. *Analysen Zur Passiven Synthesis. Aus Vorlesungs- Und Forschungsmanuskripten 1918–1926*. edited by M. Fleischer. Den Haag: Martinus Nijhoff.

Husserl, Edmund. 1973. *Zur Phänomenologie Der Intersubjektivität, Dritter Teil*, edited by I. Kern. Den Haag: Martinus Nijhoff.

Latour, Bruno. 2005. 'From Realpolitik to Dingpolitik or How to Make Things Public'. Pp. 14–42 in *Making Things Public: Atmospheres of Democracy*, edited by B. Latour and P. Weibel. Cambridge, MA: MIT Press.

Lawson, Tony. 1987. 'The Relative/Absolute Nature of Knowledge and Economic Analysis'. *The Economic Journal* 97(388):951. https://doi.org/10.2307/2233082.

Lee, Nam-In. 2002. 'Static-Phenomenological and Genetic-Phenomenological Concept of Primordiality in Husserl's Fifth Cartesian Meditation'. *Husserl Studies* 18(3):165–83. https://doi.org/10.1023/A:1020470220096.

Merleau-Ponty, Maurice. 2002. *Phenomenology of Perception*. London; New York: Routledge.

Rosa, Hartmut. 2019. *Resonance: A Sociology of the Relationship to the World*. Medford, MA: Polity Press.

Schütz, Alfred. 1996. *Collected Papers Volume IV*. The Hague: Martinus Nijhoff.

Svetlova, Ekaterina. 2008. *Sinnstiftung in der Ökonomik: wirtschaftliches Handeln aus sozialphilosophischer Sicht*. Bielefeld: transcript.

Unger, Roberto Mangabeira, and Lee Smolin. 2015. *The Singular Universe and the Reality of Time: A Proposal in Natural Philosophy*. Cambridge: Cambridge University Press.

3 Agents, institutions and the horizontal gap[1]

Based on the understanding of social reality as a process of sense-making in relation to a singular and tangible lifeworld, the question arises of who actually lives and determines these processes in concrete situations. This question has been and continues to be approached in very diverse ways by the social sciences. With regard to economic matters, much debate is carried out at the margins. Here, with the help of a maximum contrast between the two extreme cases of methodological individualism and methodological holism, a spectrum will be offered. The comparison with both positionings will then make it possible to outline a third approach.

Critique of methodological individualism

Methodological individualism, going back to Schumpeter (cf. Blaug 1992:45), is one of the basic positions in standard economics but also one of the implicit standards of numerous heterodox or other social science approaches. According to this approach, social aggregates up to entire economies are handled as sums of their individual parts. For methodological individualists, 'sociality' is never more than an aggregate, has no reality of its own and, hence, never develops its own dynamics.[2] Sociality, in the sense of a sphere or phenomenon that is independent of individuals, can thus never become an object of study for methodological individualists. This also means that such a non-existent sociality (or culture) cannot have any effect on or even shape the individual. The individual is fully explicable and determinable from within (cf. Hodgson 2004:16, 2013:2). In this respect, there is also no tension between the imagined individual and an imagined society or between the individual and the lifeworld. The relationship between the individual, sociality and the lifeworld in methodological individualism could be depicted as follows (see Figure 3.1):

DOI: 10.4324/9781003371687-3

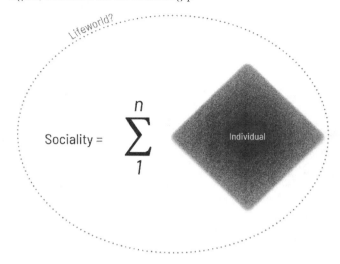

Figure 3.1 The relationship between individuality, sociality and lifeworld in methodological individualism

Methodological individualism will now be further elaborated on and deconstructed in confrontation with three central critiques:

1) Against the background from the previous chapter, an important, yet rarely discussed point is the fact that a relationship of the modelled individual to the experiential lifeworld is generally absent. The individual not only forms the basis for what one could call 'aggregated sociality', but is modelled as a self-originating entity in a radical sense. The individual of methodological individualism simply *is* and needs no other to be. For instance, it does not need a lifeworldly situatedness in order to hold and maintain its individuality or its individual predispositions. Not only 'sociality' or 'culture' form a void, but also the place and time of individuality. The neoclassical individual, for example, is a thoroughly abstract one. It does not have to refer to anything; does not have to (re)create meaning. It exists in the mind of the scientist in a complete determination.[3] In this way, methodological individualism commonly misses the core of what still constitutes the most radical individuality and determines it as such: a relationship to and within the lifeworld. Such a relationship can never be determined from a singular entity, but only in relational categories.

A methodological individualism is thus fundamentally susceptible to *ontologisations* of the human condition. Due to the methodological presupposition that explanations for human thought and action, as well as their effects, can only be explained from within the individual but never from social or lifeworldly references, a methodological individualist is necessarily dependent on *assigning* a certain individuality to the modelled individual as a constitutive starting point. This is generally achieved through the external attribution (by scientists) of characteristics or activities in the form of assumptions. Without a certain degree of anthropological definition (*Setzung*), modelling would not be possible. And it is precisely this defining activity that turns methodological individualism *en passant* into a 'metaphysical individualism' (Dewey 1939:64) or an 'ontological individualism' (Hodgson 2013:33). Here, individuality is not just used as a methodological category, but is actually being filled, and thus shaped, as a certain individuality. In the model of *homo economicus*, for example, as in the models of many other *homines*,[4] being human is not understood as an open process but as a fact, or is at least implicitly factualised (cf. Archer 2000:68).

The trap of ontological individualism, ironically, affects both parties in the debate about the unrealistic nature of the *homo economicus* model, which has been brought up again recently and is now being fought out in particular between behavioural economists and neoclassical microeconomists (Avtonomov and Avtonomov 2019; cf. Camerer and Loewenstein 2004). While the former claim that the model is wrong with reference to laboratory experiments with real people, the latter retreat to Friedman's (1953) position that it *must be* wrong in order to produce relevant predictions. Inherent in both positions, however, is that they make ontologising statements about human beings – how they *are*, in order to make them manageable methodically, or how they *actually* or *really* are. According to such an understanding, the economic agent is absorbed in characteristics or dispositions to which he cannot create any distance. In this aspect, a modelled human being who cannot establish any distance to his preference order or utility function matches the real human being who cannot establish any distance to his experimentally studied behaviour patterns. Both 'humans' are attested a being by scientists, which is (or can be) expanded into metaphysical anthropologies. And in both cases, this ontologising attribution may be interpreted as an expression of an understanding of science oriented towards being and not becoming: "the original sin of mainstream economics is its putting at the beginning the subject–object relationship, as if the object was always already fully constituted when the always already fully constituted subject approaches it" (Dupuy 2004:276).

2) Methodological individualism in its concrete standard economic form is also problematic or contradictory with regard to its (mostly implicit) concept of freedom. Although the individual is modelled as a potent

decision-maker, he or she cannot decide either not to decide at all or to decide on the basis of a self-chosen rationality or will. The modelled individual is only free up to the limits of the model. It is a slave to its decision-making calculus given to it by the modeller (cf. Hodgson 1988:17, 99, see also 2003:170; Loasby 2007:190–91; Jackson 2009:129). This compulsion to decide is closely related to its ontologised status and the (functional) properties attributed to it in the modelling process. George Shackle summarises the underlying programmatic aspect as follows: "Conventional economics is not about choice, but about acting according to necessity. Economic man obeys the *dictates of reason*, follows the *logic of choice*" (Shackle 1949:272; cit. as in Loasby 2007:190). Here, the limits of the understanding of rationality immanent in economic modelling become apparent, which is closely linked to the rationality of the modelling scientist him/herself (cf. Mirowski 1987:1003–05). In order to be methodically manageable and controllable, the rationality and freedom of decision-making of the modelled agents can only ever be conceded up to a limit of calculability. Thinking or decision-making beyond the model or other forms of practice can only be gained and reconstructed by abandoning this methodical decision.

3) Finally, the thorny question of the concept of the 'individual' inherent in methodological individualism has to be addressed. It becomes fragile not only against the background of the loss of a capacity for free decision-making – that is, for agency – but, in fact, the standard economic concept of the individual is said to lack what has been an essential criterion of individuality ever since Aristotle; namely, some form of distinguishability of one individual from another (cf. Davis 2003:14, 43, 2011:5, 15). The modelled individual of standard economics, however, not only lacks any distinguishability from possible other individuals but also a distinction from other modelled units (such as firms or states), which are also only represented in the form of a utility function: utility-maximising choice decisions follow a "general, all-purpose logic that could be applied to any sort of agent, single individual, multi-individual, human, or otherwise" (Davis 2003:26). And, even if a residual form of individuality were to be created through different formal programming (e.g., in the form of different utility functions or preference orders), there would still remain a complete identity in the *modus operandi* of 'individual' decisions: all are identical in that they operate on the basis of a formal attribution. Fundamental differences, as they become manifest in lived social practice – for example, in historical or cultural specificities or in practices that go beyond existing systems of rules – cannot be negotiated under such methodological conditions.

In this reading, it seems doubtful whether methodological individualists do justice at all to the inherent criteria of their own basic methodological positioning (cf. Davis 2003, sec. 2.2). There is no doubt that this deficit largely stems from a model Platonism taken to the extremes (cf. Albert 1963) and a concomitant 'dehumanisation' of economic theorisation (cf. Giocoli 2003:3; Mirowski 2002). Mirowski (cf. 2002:441) proposes the term 'methodological cyborgism' for this post-human shift in the methodological positioning of economic theory since WWII. Martin Hollis sums up the post-human character of the standard economic view of man: "If we recall that preferences are given, then it will be seen that the agent is simply a throughput" (Hollis 1988:68). The narrative of the rational utility maximiser shows itself to be misleading here in that it suggests a reference to actual humanness, which is, however, counteracted by the methodological operationalisation in all essential aspects of the human condition (see the following explanations). A crucial facet of being human is precisely the uniqueness of each person in his or her existential relationship to other people and the lifeworld. It is this uniqueness that is not preserved in the dominant varieties of methodological individualism, of all things, but must be prevented so that the methodical operations become possible at all.

Taken together, the above arguments underline that, despite the centrality of individuality and freedom in contemporary economic thinking (cf. Davis 2003:1; Düppe 2009:67), the need for a different approach to human agency in economics is essential.

Critique of methodological holism

The other extreme of social science research approaches can be seen in methodological holism, which has also been called methodological collectivism or functionalism. It takes as its starting point the explanation of social phenomena exclusively on the basis of social structures, against the background of which individuals appear, at best, as a part or expression but never as a determining factor. As Margaret Archer has pointed out, this analytical approach can be found especially in postmodern social theories (Archer 2000:3; see also Davis 2003:1.2).

The image of the human being present in this tradition dissolves into social structures in which a single individual no longer has an identity of his or her own: "A self does not amount to much" (Lyotard 1984:15). Archer emphasises that at least postmodern theoretical approaches often identify social structures with language or discourse. The individual breaks down into the discourses in which he or she participates. Social structures or processes, in the context of a methodological holism, exert a total effect on individuals so that they disappear into social structures to the limit of their dissolution. A 'structural determinism'

(Archer 2000:29) defines the position and colouring of the individual, an effect from which it is impossible to distance or even detach itself:

> Individuals are not themselves constitutive of the social process or history but are only its träger, and that the consciousness or subjectivity of the subject is constructed in ideology. The former insists that we are not the 'makers of history' but only the supporting material which energises the process.
>
> (Archer 2000:28)

The complete subordination or even dissolution of the individual into social structures could be approximated in the following figure (Figure 3.2):

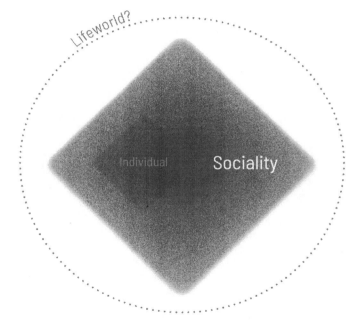

Figure 3.2 The relationship between individuality, sociality and lifeworld in methodological holism

Interestingly, there is a close parallel between this individual dissolving into a sociality and the third point of criticism with reference to methodological individualism. Just as a distinctive understanding of individuality begins to dissolve in a functional assignment assumed for all modelled human beings, so, too, in methodological holism does the individual dissolve in assumed social structures. Although these are generally not mathematically preconfigured, verbal forms of the pre-stabilisation or predetermination of individuals exist here as well.

Another remarkable parallel to methodological individualism is the complete identification of the signified with the sign. In other words, methodological holism harbours the danger of metaphysical holism. In this extreme position, there is no longer any lifeworld 'out there', and thus, no longer any relations to something non-social or genuinely other:

> 'Signs lose contact with things signified; the late twentieth century is witness to unprecedented destruction of meaning. The quest for some division between the moral and the immoral, the real and the unreal is futile' (Lyon 1994:16). There 'is nothing which *has* these interpretations, just as there is no uninterpreted reality these are interpretations of' (Guignon/Hiley 1996, 344).
>
> (Archer 2000:32, 34)

Just as methodological individualism tends towards a metaphysical individualism and, in this exaggeration, forgets everything genuinely other from which individuality can develop in the first place, methodological holism is also marked by an oblivion of the lifeworld through the exuberant allocation of meaning in the direction of social structures and systems. Language, signs, institutions, etc. are all that there is – they no longer refer to something genuinely different. Both – methodological individualism and methodological holism – are interested in the identification of permanent causalities. The identification and arrangement of these causalities lead to sometimes-complex systems of modes of action, which are then able to describe or even predict certain states of these systems. The decisive characteristic of these systems is that they are *self-referential*, insofar as they need no other to make sense. Even if rhetorical references to other systems or even the lifeworld are sometimes built up, they do not need this in order to claim validity within the system of relevance they are establishing.

Seen from a phenomenological perspective, these approaches must necessarily remain meaningless because their interest in knowledge is not directed precisely at the world and the relationships established in it, which makes them possible in the first place and in which they realise their research. Neither individuals (as attempted by methodological individualism) nor social entities or structures (as attempted by methodological holism) can meaningfully attain an explanatory capacity of the lifeworld *out of themselves*. For this reason, a fundamentally different path will be taken here.

Institutional agency

The inadequacies of methodological individualisms and holisms call for alternative approaches and procedures in social science research when it comes to the question of *who* actually makes sense of the lifeworld. One of the central criteria in such an undertaking is the consistent avoidance of ontologisations of social processes, including the self-referentiality of modelled systems of thought (cf. Hodgson 2004:29). Instead of using the methodological framework to literally anticipate research results and assign their origin to static individualities or socialities, a framework is needed that enables a methodically controlled and comprehensible examination of the question of how people jointly approach the previously described problem of interpreting lifeworldly situations. In such an analytical setting, individuality as well as sociality are not questions of being, but of becoming.[5] As I already made clear in the previous chapter, social and thus also economic reality is introduced here as a process of social sense-making, related to and embedded in the tangible lifeworld. Following the institutionalist tradition, this framing is now concretised. In my opinion, institutionalism is able to preserve the fundamental openness of sense-making processes and, at the same time, offer methodically controlled ways of dealing with them scientifically.

People are never blank slates. They speak, act, play, make decisions in the context and in relation to a lifeworld based on inherited patterns and conventions that they learn in the course of their lives:

> The extent to which people have a need for meanings and explanations in their everyday lives is often underestimated. In all cultures known to anthropology, there is evidence of the universal human hunger for meaning. It is fed by religion, by ritual, through playful curiosity or by modern science. In meeting our desire for meaning, we acquire the habits of thought and behaviour of our culture.
>
> (Hodgson 2003:168)

> The means of understanding the world are necessarily acquired through social relationships and interactions. Cognition is a social as well as an individual process. Individual choice is impossible without these institutions and interactions.
>
> (Hodgson 2013:38)

Hodgson introduces a social concept of knowledge that human sense-making is always a socially shared process. This applies, on the one hand, to the *content* of meanings in the form of languages, rules, manners, etc., but also to the *process* of their appropriation and reproduction. These processes are social in nature, insofar as they have their constitutive place in the interaction of living people (cf. Spong 2019:5). For the social frameworks or patterns of sense-making, the concept of *institutions* shall be introduced:

> We may define institutions broadly as durable systems of established and embedded social rules that structure social interactions. The term 'rule' is

broadly understood as an injunction or disposition that in circumstances X do Y.

(Hodgson 2004:14)

Institutions are thus codifiable systems of rules in and of social contexts that are interactively (re)produced by the participants in these contexts (cf. Fleetwood 2008b:244). Thrown into a family, group, milieu, language family, and/or society, agents learn these groups' specific rules of interpreting and dealing with the lifeworld. They may be more (e.g., laws, codified rules) or less (e.g., taboos or routines) explicitly presented or reflected. Scott (cf. 2014:56–57) distinguishes on such a spectrum of explicit codification of rule systems, for example, between regulative, normative and cultural-cognitive institutions (cf. in detail my own proposal along a vertical axis in the following chapter). In their interplay, institutions allow for a relatively stable (re)production of social references to the lifeworld; they "provide stability and meaning to social life" (Scott 2014:56). In the context of a decidedly praxeological approach and contrary to an exclusively mentalistic understanding of institutions, it must be emphasised that lived social practices and their products always find a material expression, *at least at the time of their performative (re)production*. After all, as enacted interpretations of the lifeworld, they are a tangible part of it. The materiality of institutions is not only evident in social interactions (e.g. in a production hall) but also in the supposedly lifeless artefacts (cf. Knorr-Cetina 1997). Tools, for example, are materialised social imaginaries, but their meaning can only be permanently maintained if they are linked to a concrete practice. In short, institutions can take on different forms or modalities. Linguistically or pictorially composed symbolic systems are just as important as social interactions or material artefacts. These different forms of institutions interlock or mutually support each other. Thus, the institution 'University of Chicago' is produced semester after semester in the interplay of designated buildings and more or less codified practices of studying, working and teaching, which in turn depend on established symbolic systems of a more or less explicit nature.

The interactive (re)production of institutions by actual, living people addresses a crucial characteristic of them, which leads to the core concept of the approach to social phenomena proposed here. Institutions[6] are always linked to agents in one and the same process - the interpretation of the lifeworld. The (re)production of institutions and agents always originates in the same process: they both emerge and endure in the lived, social process of sense-making. Thus, the object of institutional analysis is the same as that of agential analysis: "If we look at social practices in one way, we can see actors and actions; if we look at them in another way we can see structures" (Craib 1992:3–4; cit. as in Davis 2003:112; see also Hodgson 2013:43).[7] "For" What we as social scientists look at in this double-sidedness, the term 'institutional agency' (Zilber 2002:236), shall now be introduced. An understanding of institutions can only be gained through the performative sense-making processes of living people (. . . *agency*), just as an understanding of agents cannot be gained without grasping their institutional history (their biography), situation (for example through a social affiliation) and their concrete ways of dealing with them (*institutional* . . .). Institutions are *enacted* by agents (cf. Weick 1979:6), and it is only in these enactments that their meaning is realised, perpetuated and/or changed (cf. Karnøe 1997:425). The concept of *institutional agency* allows one to conceive of social reality as "simultaneously given and made" (Jaeggi 2018:350). In institutional economics, this double character leading, in fact, to a research approach on *institutionalisations* rather than *institutions* is, partly, inspired by Anthony Giddens' structuration theory (Davis 2003:112; cf. Hodgson 2004:30–32). The supposedly contradictory poles of agents and institutions are both always part of the same social fact. The methodological decision to elevate only one of these poles to the rank of explanatory power is arbitrary and does not do justice to the potentiality and reality of social processes (cf. Lawson 1987:969). Just as institutions only come into being through their realisation by living people, people are always already dependent on institutions in order to survive (Dolfsma and Verburg 2008:1034; Fleetwood 2008a:243; Fullbrook 2002; Hodgson 2002:173, cf. 2013:41; Jackson 1999; Wrenn 2015:1232). Most importantly, it must always be remembered that the poles of sociality and individuality are not mediated somewhere, but in the tangible lifeworld. The (re)production of institutional arrangements through human interactions takes place in and in relation to a concrete historical and spatial situation:

> Crucial for the analysis here is the elemental recognition that all institutional forms, behavioural or attitudinal, are products of *the world of experience*. Institutions do not originate in heaven, with Mother Nature, or with any other outside-of-experience force. . . . Institutions of whatever kind are people-made devices for organizing experience and thus, by obvious inference, they are always potentially modifiable by people.
>
> (Tool 1985:74; my emphasis)

A somewhat 'naked' analysis of institutionalisations that overlooks the fact that institutions only appear, are handed down and changed because actual people already refer to them and have to refer to them in a tangible situation would therefore miss the point. Social reality emerges in the messy interrelationship between agents, social structures (i.e., institutions) and the lifeworld (cf. Baggio 2020:1670).

It should be pointed out in this context that the relationships people form with the lifeworld on the basis of institutions include not only the situational setting, fellow human beings and nature, but also the very people themselves. What has already been introduced about relations to the lifeworld also applies to *self-relationships*. They always take place on the basis of institutionalised rules, images and language: "The individual is not taken as given, but situated within an interactive social context that enables her education and development" (Baggio 2020:1671; see Hodgson 2002:174–75, 2013:24). Spong (2019:9), following John B. Davis, calls these self-related institutions 'self-concepts' and outlines that the formation, stabilisation and change of a self is always a process that takes place through institutions (cf. Lawlor 2006:330; Spong 2019:3–4). Spong (2019:9) also speaks of self-relationships as a continuous 'self-transformation' on the basis of social institutions, for instance, in the form of inner dialogues (cf. Fuller 2013:123). Being a self thus appears as an institutional (a fundamentally social) relationship and becoming a self as a process of institutionalisation. In any case, it cannot be described as always already being or always being the same. Schematically, the above-mentioned process of institutionalised human references to the lifeworld – which also include self-relationships – could be represented as follows (see Figure 3.3). The left-hand rhombus of agents forms an overlapping area with the right-hand rhombus of social structures, in which individuality and sociality coincide in the concept of *institutional agency*.

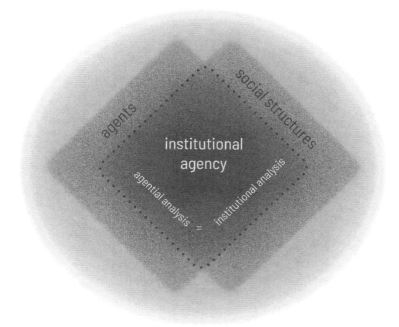

Figure 3.3 The relationship between individuality, sociality and lifeworld

Subjectivation, a.k.a. institutionalisation

Now that the concept of institutional agency has, so to speak, marked out the playing field of those processes on which social reality is negotiated and (re) produced, possible directions of these (re)production processes must be identified. A first direction is that of the continuation of existing institutions. In accordance with the double relationship between institutions and agents just introduced, this process of institutional reproduction is described both as subjectivation (through and in agents) and as institutionalisation (in the fabric of social structures).

Subjectivation here means learning institutional patterns – a process that changes the agents themselves.[8] The decisive point is that subjectivation always refers to the *adaptation* or *consolidation* of social patterns, irrespective of the *mode* of adaptation (cf. Chapter 4). In order to better understand what is hidden behind the concept of subjectivation, the concept of habituation will first be introduced as an auxiliary bridge:

> I define habituation as the process through which institutions (rules, conventions, norms, values and customs) become internalised and embodied within agents, generating the dispositions we call habits or *habitus*. It seems to me that the process of habituation involves the following three (main) processes:
>
> (i)   Repetition, regularity, routinization and continuity. The (let us say) rule-guided agent finds herself repeating the same action over some extended period. . . .
>
> (ii) Reinforcement, or incentive and disincentive. There are positive and negative reinforcements to engaging in rule-guided action, such as approval or disapproval by members of the appropriate community. . . .
>
> (iii) Intimacy, familiarity or close proximity. To internalise or embody institutions (rules conventions, norms, values and customs) the agent has to engage with them, live with them and use them, until agents feel 'like a fish in water', as it is commonly put.
>
> It is via these three (main) processes of habituation that institutions and agents are linked.
>
> (Fleetwood 2008a:249)

Fleetwood lists three possible ways in which the implicit institutions (rules, habits, norms, values, etc.) of a community, group, milieu, society, language family, generation, etc. are internalised by the agents involved in them and, to a certain extent, perpetuate and stabilise the respective institutional structure. These processes are certainly gradual in nature and can sometimes take on 'hard' and thus more organised forms, such as those found in manipulation or indoctrination (cf. Hodgson 2003:168). But they can also take on soft forms, in which rules are presented in social life without noticeable effort and are internalised just as smoothly by those participating. This may be especially true for areas such as the acquisition of the mother tongue or learning how to handle money. Herbert Mead used the metaphor of a game to illustrate these social learning processes, in which agents learn from childhood on, through practical participation in the social play, according to which rules others play, how they are likely to behave accordingly and which roles and practices are interlinked in the game (Baggio 2020:1389; cf. Mead 2000:152–64). If one looks at these processes from the side of social structures, they could also be described as *institutionalisations*. The performative repetition of rule systems by agents leads to institutional consolidation and continuity (cf. Zucker 1977).

Hodgson (2002:168) has introduced the term 'reconstitutive downward causation' for this form of institutional persistence. 'Reconstitutive' insofar as this imprinting 'from above', or more precisely, 'from the right' – i.e., the social structures and agents themselves – are also changed (cf. direction of arrow from right to left in Figure 3.4). The process of habitualisation works through agents, insofar as they realise the institutions. In this facet as being permeated by social institutions right into their own self-relations, human beings can be

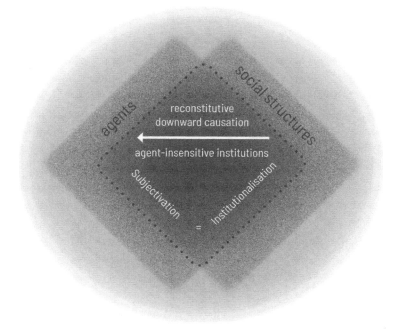

Figure 3.4 Institutionalisations or subjectivations as reconstitutive downward causation

described as *subjects.*[9] And the day-by-day process within which people develop in their self-relationships on the basis of social institutions is called *subjectivation.* Processes of institutionalisation are always processes of subjectivation, insofar as the agents who realise them also develop in the process:

> We start from the contention that socio-economic systems do not simply create new products and perceptions. *They also create and re-create individuals.* The individual not only changes his/her purposes and preferences, but also revises his/her skills and his/her perceptions of his/her needs.
> (Fleetwood 2008b:184; cf. also Hodgson 2002:168, 172, 2003:162)

From the agent's point of view, new ways of interpreting and dealing with things are learned, but without the latter changing with the agent. Due to the primacy of the institution over the agent, the term 'agent-insensitive institution' (Hodgson 2004:438) has been introduced as a respective institutional concept of subjectivation. Within the framework of institutionalisations, existing systems of rules are reproduced; they are not changed, or at least, not significantly. In this context, the commonly negatively connoted facets of institutions must also be seen as stabilising factors for the privileges of certain groups or individuals. Institutional change then appears as a power issue that is prevented by those who benefit from the privileges associated with established institutions. However, these institutional restrictions or intensities are not natural but social in nature (cf. Tool 1985:166; Hodgson 2002:176, 2003; Beckert 2010:616–17; Zilber 2002:237).

Self-transformation, aka. institutional transformation

From what has been said so far, the impression could be given that people – as also laid out in methodological holism, for example – are always subjected to institutional structures or even determined by them. Individuals would then completely dissolve into institutional arrangements, and one could fully understand a person if one had deciphered his or her institutional biography. Such a perspective would therefore explain institutional change with reference only to institutions because individuals would only appear as 'bearers', but not as shapers of them. While institutionalism has always, in critical distinction from neoclassical mainstream, emphasised and sometimes prioritised structures,[10] the relationship between agents and institutions must now be specified. This will also reveal the potential of institutional transformation arising from the interplay between agents and institutions.

As already introduced, institutions are the socially shared ways of dealing with the lifeworld in concrete situations by actual people. Social life is always carried on by living people; they bring institutions into being through their actions: "The basic element in society is not the abstract individual, but the social individual, one who is both constructive within and constructed through society" (Hodgson 1988:71).

The question of institutional change must therefore inevitably start with the social interactions of living people; the place of (re)production of institutions as ways of dealing with the lifeworld is the interaction of people.

The evident reality of an emergence of new institutions – for example, in the form of new routines or collective self-images – proves that both structures and agents are alterable and, at least potentially, without absolute limits. Their actual limits lie rather in the social acceptance or permeability of new social imaginaries. This also addresses the issue of power relations and socio-economic preconditions for change. Not everyone has an interest in change and in the reconfiguration of social relations. A static society, for example, would be one in which social imaginaries are seen as absolutely unchanging. Eugen Fink (1970:104) speaks of "closed societies" in this context. A conception of subjectivity related to this concept was put forward by Norbert Elias (1998) in his *homo clausus*. At the same time, however, one can learn from both authors that such archetypes of sociality or subjectivity are historical and by no means necessary. In demarcation from such static and congealing images of social processes, I follow Archer in her wish for the reorientation of social science research around the practice of actual, living people: "I wish to reclaim human beings as the ultimate *fons et origio* of (emergent) social life or socio-cultural structures" (Archer 2000:18). It then becomes clear that "in society and culture everything that seems fixed is simply frozen politics or interrupted struggle. The inventions, the conflicts, and the compromises, in thought and in practice, are all there is; there is nothing else" (Unger 2007:33). Social realities are produced by people and can therefore always be changed by people. Social reality is not the product of ontologised processes or entities working miraculously in the background but the intermediate result of social interactions in relation to the lifeworld.

This raises questions about the extent to which individuals can be differentiated from institutions and whether and how individuals can possibly change institutional systems of rules themselves. These questions have been dealt with in very different ways in institutionalism. I will argue and justify a position that emphasises the uniqueness and creative power of the individual (. . . *agency*) without undermining its institutional embeddedness (*institutional* . . .). In the following, I will refer to this genuine power of the individual pole as *individual potentiality*. The related concept is that of *social potentiality*. Impulses for institutional change can also emanate from the social pole (but never without agents realising this potentiality). Both potentialities are ultimately an expression of a fundamental difference between agents and social structures; these poles can never be completely dissolved into each other. For this non-identity of agents and social structures, I introduce the concept of the *horizontal gap* (cf. Figure 3.5).

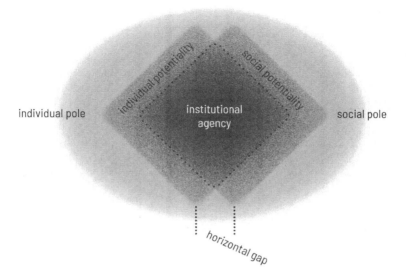

Figure 3.5 The non-identity of individuality and sociality and the resulting potential for social transformation

Individual potentiality

The sources of individual potentiality discussed here are threefold, and all point to the uniqueness of the individual. Seen from the individual pole, the question of the possibilities of institutional change is identical with the question of the distinctiveness of each individual person. In relation to the terminology just introduced, this means that the human being is never completely absorbed into the subject and can never be conclusively determined when his or her institutional biography is decoded. In this way, the position proposed here places itself in the tradition of Aristotelean anthropology (cf. Davis 2011:5). Three arguments, or sources, for the reality of an individual potentiality and uniqueness are now introduced. These arguments are not attributions or inscriptions of individuality from the outside (cf. Davis 2003:12) but sketches of fields of possibility in which individuality can freely unfold.

1)   *Body*[11]

The phenomenologically evident fact that every living human being has a body forms the first argument for the uniqueness and potentiality of the individual. In neoclassical theorising, the physical condition of the human being is completely absent (cf. Amariglio and Ruccio 2001:143–46). That which is modelled as an 'individual' for methodological reasons is completely absorbed by a mathematical operation that solves maximisation problems, like a computer (cf. Ötsch 2019:255–59). A striking blossom of this complete abstraction from the human body is the fact that standard economic modelling usually focuses exclusively on the moment of decision-making between given alternatives (to be optimised) – but not on the reality and the consequences that arise from this decision. The famous textbook example is that of the consumption of ice-cream scoops, which is not constrained by full or satisfied stomachs or bodies but by a quantum of utility emanating from the consumption of ice-cream in relation to an available budget (cf. Mankiw 2021:63–66).[12] The sometimes-complex corporeality that forms a constitutive condition of *every* lived economic action and relationship must give way, in this tradition, to the methodological motivations of economists working in the tradition of a disembodied *cogito*. Without its body, however, there would undoubtedly be no publicly visible self. An 'institutional agency' is, at the same time, always an 'embodied agency' (Taylor 1989a). Through its existence, it is perceived as a human being and thus also forms – qua continuity in appearance – the basis for the change of the self in the instituting process (cf. Antony 2017; Archer 2000:39).[13] With reference to Merleau-Ponty, Archer introduces the recognition of the human being's bodily condition as a bridge between phenomenology and critical realism:

> For both realism and phenomenology, we are thrown into the real world and make what we can of situations, of which we have no prior understanding, through exercising our species' endowments in praxis. . . . It is the body which constitutes the anchorage of our perceptual limitations and affordances. Thus, it is from the body that the 'perceiving subject must, without relinquishing his place and his point of view, and in the opacity of sensation, reach out towards things to which he has, in advance no key, and for which he nevertheless carries within himself the project, and open himself to an absolute Other which he is making ready in the depths of his being.' [M. Merleau-Ponty, *The Phenomenology of Perception*, Routledge and Kegan Paul, London, 1962, p. 326.]
>
> (Archer 2000:127)

It is thus part of the human condition to always perceive in one's own bodily experience an insurmountable difference to the 'absolute Other'. From the first palpations of the lifeworld as an infant, we relate to our environment in an existence that is always also bodily constituted (cf. Archer 2000:147). And, in the resistance which confronts us by touching, feeling and sensually perceiving, a bodily induced difference to the phenomenal setting is marked at the same time (cf. Archer 2000:130, 153, 2003:119–20). The development of an individuality is thus constitutively dependent on the experience and contact with the genuinely other; it originates in the lifeworldly situated and bodily bound human experience (cf. Saito 1991:22, 25). Our body marks the absolute standpoint in and from which we have to approach the lifeworld, and our points of view simultaneously reveal our bodily-bound uniqueness, which can be exchanged in movement, discourse or imagination, but never dissolved (cf. Bäuerle 2019; Davis 2003:143). From there also stems the body's potentiality: it indicates a spatio-temporally unique standpoint that cannot be taken by any other. This also applies in a figurative sense to the standpoints and experiences that a person takes in the course of his or her life. The body-bound development is not only valid for a certain moment but also forms an essential facet of a biographical becoming. Throughout our lives, we do not lose our bodily condition. The body is thus also unique in its historical dimension. No one else could experience and perceive what could be experienced and perceived from this body. However, the body's uniqueness in the historical dimension applies equally to the wealth of experiences made in the course of a life and the reflections on these experiences. Finally, the body is a testimony to this spatio-temporal uniqueness. Aspects of our lives manifest themselves in it, such as our age, what form of life we have chosen so far and how we place ourselves in the world in the form of clothing, styling, surgical procedures, etc.

2) Unique experiences

From an institutional point of view, the individual's uniqueness is further indicated by his or her specific institutional experiences throughout life. In the first place, it does not matter whether these experiences were undergone more or less consciously. The institutional experiences that people gather in the course of their lives in concrete situations are reflected in the skills and habits that have been learned in those social settings, such as milieus, groups, etc. (Davis 2003:144; cf. Lawlor 2006:336). To a certain extent, they are the more or less successfully realised possibilities of interpreting and dealing with the lifeworld. From such a point of view, it is impossible for two individuals to have developed with and through the same institutions.[14] Commonalities shared by belonging to one group or milieu are contrasted in each agent by differences stemming from belonging to other groups, milieus or other institutionalised ways of dealing with the lifeworld (cf. Karnøe 1997:425). Here, too, individuality shows itself once again in relation to otherness and to different othernesses, in each case. In the course of our lives, we all talk to different people, engage in different situations and belong to various groups.

This combination of unique influences therefore also extends to the development and shaping of our self-interpretations (cf. Spong 2019:4, 7). Self-transformation also takes place on the basis of a unique combination of institutional arrangements and decisions. In this respect, the process and the content of the process coincide; a unique self-transformation takes place on the basis of unique possibilities and circumstances. In the realisation of this process, a distinctive personality emerges. The experiences realised up to now and the sense-making procedures learned in them enable each individual person to create new possibilities of sense-making from their specific biography and specific mix of skills and knowledge. Here, too, it is initially irrelevant whether these possibilities are seized more or less consciously. What matters is that specific possibilities of sense-making emerge through the unique biography of individual agents.

The simple example of a situation that is experienced by two people together and is evaluated, interpreted, processed and approached differently by both people on the basis of respective social imaginaries shows very clearly that the *interpretation* of a situation is just as little identical with the situation as the *individual way of dealing with it*. This also means that two individuals can never 'stand' in the same place through a supposedly complete overlap of their positioning in a situation because, as living human beings, they bring with them a distinctive biography in relation to other people: "In explicitly recognising that agents make differing interpretations, evaluations, and choices within the same context, Archer's approach can offer a recognition of individuality that does not rely upon positional difference" (Spong 2019:9). Beyond the positional difference already introduced above by the bodily self, there is always an institutional difference that distinguishes every human being from every other human being.[15] The fact that this difference by no means just 'happens' to the human being but can be induced by the person in the decision itself forms a third facet of human distinctiveness and potentiality.

3) Freedom to transform institutions

Both forms of institutional transformation vouch for the individual's potentiality to transcend one's social bonds and create new relationships towards the lifeworld. Individual agents are not only uniquely shaped but can also potentially have a uniquely formative impact (cf. Archer 2000:49). Hodgson introduced the concept of *reconstitutive upward causation* as a counter concept to *reconstitutive downward causation*. In the graphic model proposed here, its direction of action runs from the left rhombus in the direction of the rhombus of social structures to the right (cf. Figure 3.6). A fundamental difference or non-identity of agents and social structures, indicated by the horizontal gap, raises this possibility of institutional transformation in the first place. However, this creative freedom always remains related to and bound in the lifeworld. Institutional change is a concrete process that can be experienced in tangible situations.

As already introduced above, self-relation also belongs to the realm of instituted relations and thus also to the realm of possible new creations of institutional arrangements. The self-relation can be thought of something like the mirror image of what is brought into being as a reference to the world. If a new relationship to the lifeworld is developed by means of the freedom given to the individual, a new self-relationship also emerges (cf. Tool 1985:54). In the realisation of the human potential for innovation, the individual simultaneously displays his or her uniqueness in a third way. The new relationship to the lifeworld created by him or her casts its shadow back on the creative agent. The unique, new relation to the world indicates a unique person. Institutional transformation, thought in this way, is always at the same time self-transformation (cf. Archer 2000:10). As already pointed out in relation to the bodily constitution of the self, the free self always shows and develops in relation to and in dependence on the lifeworld. The uniqueness of the self cannot be established without the non-self called lifeworld. Positively formulated: The self develops its unique dealings in relation to something that precedes and transcends it. And the unique product of this creative reference – the new institution – is also bound to the lifeworld from the moment of its realisation onwards. Self and institution spring from one and the same active process and both sides expand the possibilities of human references to the lifeworld. They push the boundaries of what can be thought, said and done and thus contribute to the abundance of institutional realities and potentialities – without, however, having come any closer to the lifeworld. The lifeworld is and remains unreachable, irrespective of the abundance of social imaginaries.

How does this individual transformational process look from the social pole? Hodgson calls institutional arrangements that are more permeable to the creative impulses of single individuals or groups *agent sensitive institutions*. The degree of this sensitivity or permeability of individual potentiality is, again, to be thought of as a spectrum: from very rigid institutional settings that prevent the creative power of agents by all means, to such institutions that cannot exist at all without the transformational praxis of individual agents. For the demarcation of an agent sensitive institution, it would be decisive that this type of institution experiences a reconfiguration through the ideas, norms and values of the individuals, which they sometimes only develop in the active process: "An *agent sensitive institution* is one in which the reigning . . . conventions can be significantly altered if the preferences or dispositions of some agents are" (Hodgson 2006:16; cit. as in Fleetwood 2008b:192; see also Spong 2019:13; Hodgson 2004:438). Agents can reconfigure the institutional structure of a lifeworldly situation through performative change, rearrangement or also through the creation of new possible social imaginaries. Not infrequently, such processes take place precisely when established institutions no longer help establish an adequate relationship towards the lifeworld (cf. Fleetwood 2008b:198; Tool 1985:172). In this case, social change originates from individuals or groups who set out to arrange or design new institutions as a result of a relationship towards the lifeworld that has become problematic; for example, in the form of environmental crises, hostilities or dysfunctionalities. At the core of the understanding of institutional transformation established here is the human capability to practically bring new institutions into being (cf. Scott 2014:60).

With the concept of freedom, we have arrived at the core of the anthropology introduced here, as well as at the core of institutional transformation. In order to approach this concept, I would first like to agree with Hodgson that there is no institutional void *in the tangible lifeworld*: "The institution free state of nature is unattainable, in minimally adequate theory as well as in reality" (Hodgson 2004:21–22, see also 2013:39, 42). Even if there were such a 'natural state', it would not be accessible to us as human beings because we would always encounter it through institutionalised – i.e., socially shared and established – forms of sense-making in the broadest sense. At the same time, however, human beings have the ability to *create* something *ex nihilo* (Beckert and Bronk 2018:2; Graupe 2020; cf. Unger 2007:7). It is possible for human beings to produce new institutions: "we are an infinite caught within the finite. The finite, in this instance, is the open series of social worlds - the formative institutional and imaginative contexts - that we construct and inhabit. The infinite is the personality" (Unger 1987:12). Human creations come out of (limitless) nothingness and, as soon as they come into the world, they become a (finite) something. In this respect, there is no place where possible institutions are 'stored' - this 'place' is human freedom and the capability to make use of it. As soon as this capability is lived out, this practice, as spatio-temporally situated, necessarily takes place in relation to the lifeworld and the established institutional structure. The realisation of this creative freedom marks a lifeworldly phenomenon that can be observed and perceived by other agents as a (new) experience of difference (cf. Dolfsma and Verburg 2008:1043). Through the inspired act, the human being thus introduces something genuinely new into what already exists. In this respect, the concept of active freedom is identical with the concept of creativity (from the Latin *creatio*: choice, creation). It is not a (natural) state but an *active process* that lies at the centre of the concept of freedom proposed here; it is 'agency freedom' (Sen 1985b:203 ff.).[16] I call the active reconstitution of existing institutional arrangements in the course of such a free process *institutional transformation* and distinguish between two forms:

a) Weak institutional transformation

People can distance themselves, to a certain extent, from the social institutions that surround them and through which they have been shaped. In this distancing, which is often identified in the literature with the concept of reflection, they can examine and evaluate their imprints, and in doing so, they already undertake a self-determined reconfiguration of the institutional structure (cf. Davis 2003:111–17, 2011:207). By whom or what was I actually shaped? Through this distancing, not only is one point of view abandoned but another is gained, through which one's own life and the institutions dominating in it are re-evaluated (cf. Fuller 2013:120–21). The decision to distance oneself marks a processual void in institutional reproduction that becomes the source of a new

relationship towards the self and the world. In relation to existing institutions, however, this form of institutional transformation remains weak.
People can also, to a certain extent, decide to change their institutional
framework: "*Within culturally specified limits* which are themselves subject to discretionary revision, a person has genuine discretion. In large
measure, people can determine 'which direction is forward'; obviously,
it is they who provide the 'stream of decisions'" (Tool 1985:86; my
emphasis). For example, at a biographical crossroads, they can decide
in favour of a certain experience, path or new social situation. Instead
of simply accepting the institutional distinctiveness introduced in (2),
agents recognise and realise the alterability of it and direct it in a chosen
direction. Another example would be the choice between two schools
with different pedagogical concepts, etc. These possibilities are cases
of weak institutional transformation, in which people opt for a creative approach to already existing institutional arrangements and thus for
their reorganisation or reconstitution. Margaret Archer, Charles Taylor
and Amartya Sen have all used the term 'commitment' for this practice:
A commitment not only indicates the concerns that agents have in the
world but, at the same time, it reveals something about their understand-
ings of themselves (cf. Archer 2000:83; Taylor 1989b:27 ff.; Sen 1977,
1985a). Within a praxeological framework, it should be pointed out that
forms of weak institutional transformation do not have to be reflexive
in nature, despite the rather decisionist vocabulary used here. Creativity
can also take on a strong performative form. An often-cited example
of performative distancing can be seen in the iterations described by
Deleuze. In the repetition of acts, people can carry out smaller or larger
changes. Marc Tool (cf. 1985:75) introduced a very similar concept with
the notion of *discreteness*, which describes (economic) action as a flow
of human decisions that can be weighed and changed again and again.

b) Strong institutional transformation

People have the possibility to temporarily suspend the given social
imaginaries and to relate to the lifeworld in completely new ways:
"We sometimes put these frameworks aside. We think and act,
incongruously and surprisingly, as if they were not for real, as if
we had merely pretended to obey them while awaiting an opportu-
nity to defy them" (Unger 1987:4).[17] Human beings possess practical
and imaginative abilities by virtue of which, as introduced above,
they can transform nothing into something. Creative processes in
this sense are not decision-making processes between given alternatives. Instead, they produce alternatives that manifest themselves as
new social realities as soon as they are 'put into the world'. At the
core of these processes sits a free human practice from which new
references can emerge. They lack a final form or a 'total script' but

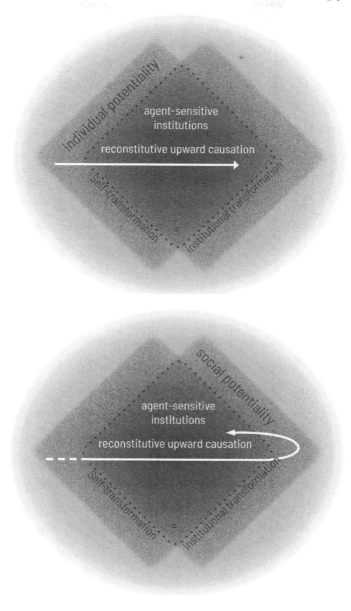

Figures 3.6 and 3.7 Self– and institutional transformation out of individual or social potentiality

are, in principle, unstable and open to continuous reinterpretation – just as this is the case, but with increasing institutional frictions, for social imaginaries shared in larger groups (cf. Davis 2011:209–10). If economics is to develop into a "volitional science, a science of the 'human will in action' [cf. Commons 1934a, 100]" (Albert and Ramstad 1997:885) it has to take seriously people's creative capacities. The decisive characteristic of strong institutional transformation is the product of the new in the process of transformation, while weak institutional transformation is always still related to the given in the creative process.[18] However, in order for this genuine newness to become manifest, it must show itself as a lifeworldly phenomenon (for example, as a discursive expression, as action, etc.). In this sense, strong institutional transformation (as a realised design process) is and remains related to the lifeworld. Even if its source lies in nothingness, institutional transformation must manifest itself as institutional transformation in the 'here and now' and trigger a socially resonating reconfiguration.

Social potentiality

Although a strong concept of individual agency is developed and presented here, the creative process is not exclusively locked in the 'genuine inner life' of an individual. On the contrary, the potential of institutional diversity and thus institutional transformation increases rapidly in the encounter of unique people. Without this encounter of living human beings, however, the potential will not be revealed. The realisation of the potentials listed below is always dependent on the practices of actual agents. Institutions cannot change institutions.[19] Institutions do not have to interpret the lifeworld, but people do. As products of human sense-making processes, institutions, and thus also processes of institutional change, are dependent on the presence and sense-making activity of living people: "[The] error is to regard institutions or social structures as if they were just things, independent of social agency" (Hodgson 2002:173). Therefore, the design of institutions must always take a diversion via social potentialities; it cannot be realised without its origin in and realisation by agents (cf. Figure 3.7).

I have already introduced the idea that even the most creative individual always undertakes his or her creations in relation to the lifeworld – i.e., in relation to something non-identical to him or her. The creative potential of this relationship can also be transferred to the relationships of difference in social interaction. In the interactions of people, different imprints, routines and ideas confront each other. In their specific reference to each other and to the lifeworld, these differences come together; for example, in the form of dialogue or war. In their cross-referencing, institutionalised procedures meet and new institutions can emerge from this encounter, which are not reducible to the institutions 'brought' into the situation. Something new emerges from social interaction. Bernhard Waldenfels describes this phenomenon using the example of a dialogue:

> If we take into account the possibility that in responding not merely an already existing meaning is reproduced, transmitted or completed, but that meaning emerges in responding itself, we encounter the paradox of a creative response in which we give what we do not have.
>
> (cit. as in Svetlova 2008:155; my translation; Waldenfels 1997:53)

This also raises the question of the actual 'agents' of this social innovation. If it is not due to individual uniqueness but to the uniqueness of the social constellation, then it arises from an intersection of several agents. To attribute social potentiality to 'the' agent in the singular is thus an impossibility, independent of the degree of awareness of mutual reference: "The co-existence with the transcendental others which is confirmed definitely by Husserl should be regarded as pre-egoistic. It is precisely because I and others in the transcendental sense co-exist at the pre-reflective level, that this co-existence is *recognised*, by *reflection*, as the *intentional* unity or *intentional* interpenetration in the reflected I" (Saito 1991:25). It is precisely this circumstance that gives rise to the sometimes-irritating diversions, which means transforming institutions via the social pole, as represented in the graphic model proposed here by a curved arrow. Without agents (left rhombus), this potentiality cannot be gained. However, they have to (temporarily) leave what is established *for them* or relativise it from the perspective of another in order to end up in an expanded field of institutional possibilities (cf. Figure 3.7).

This form of social potentiality is present *as a potential* in every social situation, thus also in *agent-insensitive institutions*. Here, too, experiences of strangeness are possible, for example, which irritate or unsettle. It may certainly have greater effects and bring about changes in the institutional setting if it is combined by the agents with individual potentialities. In this case, people proactively engage with strangers in order to explore and develop new references to the lifeworld: "The stranger as a radical break, as nonsense is no longer excluded (ignored), but recognised as a productive and constitutive component of the process of sense-making" (Svetlova 2008:152). Every encounter with the stranger brings new potentials of interpretation, which can unfold in a coincidental overlap or mixture, or in a deliberative co-creation (cf. Voorberg, Bekkers, and Tummers 2015). It is precisely this institutional diversity in the experience of alienness that Hodgson addresses when he specifies the distinction between social structures and agents as follows:

> The differentiation of structure from agent is valid if structure is seen as external to any given individual, but not if it is regarded as external to all individuals. Structure does not exist apart from all individuals, but it may exist apart from any given individual.
>
> (Hodgson 2004:36)

As in the field of individual potentialities, the boundaries of institutionalised references in social interaction are thus expanded – without, however, coming closer to the lifeworld in a fundamental sense or even catching up with it. In the required brevity, three fields or sources of experiences of otherness and thus of social potentiality should be named here:

a) *Shift in space*

In German, '*die Fremde*' (the foreign) is close to '*die Ferne*' (the remote). In these terms, a close relationship of a shift in space and experiences of otherness is implied. Elsewhere, new references to the lifeworld as carried out by strangers can be perceived. The classic example would be that of a journey to a hitherto unknown country. The notorious 'culture shock' is an expression of the irritation that such experiences of otherness can trigger (cf. Spong 2019:14).

b) *Shift in time*

The perception of one's current position in the spatio-temporal event as one that has already been occupied by someone else before and will possibly be occupied again by someone else later already points in the spatial dimension to the social potentiality inherent in the same position at another time. Who might have stood here before? How might the place have looked to him or her? What differences and developments might the specific place have undergone since then? The confrontation with the past (Bögenhold 2020; O'Sullivan 2021) or the imagination of possible futures (Beckert 2016; Miller 2018) is also a source of the experience of otherness, in which the familiar and the established are put into perspective. The cultural-historical confrontation – for example, with the established institutions in lifeworldly situations of the past – holds a great wealth of social potentiality. However, this can only be raised and, to a certain extent, updated if it is brought into a living relationship with the present: "Sense-making means making connections between the old and the new" (Svetlova 2008:139). And one could add: within the present.

c) *Artefacts*

Another source of social potentiality lays with artefacts – i.e., the material manifestations of established ways of dealing with the lifeworld. Technical equipment, clothing or buildings as examples of such artefacts have a supporting function for the established institutions of a group or society – as parts of the same– on the one hand. In a laying battery, for example, only very specific forms of keeping chickens can be realised. Their sheer existence favours the practices envisaged by them – or at least makes others less likely. But, on the other hand, artefacts are not simply there but possess referential character to *other* possible references to the lifeworld (cf. Knorr-Cetina 1997; Knorr-Cetina and Bruegger 2000). Strictly speaking, it does not matter whether the contexts of their origin are 'correctly' recognised. What is decisive for the dynamics of institutional transformation is that they differ from established institutions and their artificial materialisation. Change thus arises, as in the case of the spatial or temporal experience of difference, not as the copy of otherness but through the connection; through the reference of the known and the unknown (cf. Karnøe 1997:427).

Synopsis: Institutional transformation as a fundamentally open process

Who is actually shaping whom? Are social structures shaped by people or people by social structures? The simple answer is: the latter is the default position of human interaction; the former is always possible. People are both shaped and capable of transforming and thus of transforming themselves at the same time (cf. Davis 2003:118–19; Spong 2019:16). Within institutional agency, people can always do something differently, produce new institutions or combine them. But they do not have to. Subjects are therefore only socially *mediated* but not socially *determined*. This applies, for example, to images of 'the economy' or discourses about 'society': they are never determined *ex ante* but are produced and updated by living people in the same performative process. Due to this principally incomplete character of the events between people and the lifeworld, a dynamic process of social change emerges. As has been shown, an institutional perspective on social co-existence that allows for uniqueness and creativity is not only possible but necessary if real phenomena of institutional transformation are to be explained (cf. Unger 1987:12). Such transformation cannot be gained without the interaction of living people through the dimensions of individual or social potentialities. This social process of sense-making, situated in the lifeworld, is the main subject of social scientists, including economists. Neither methodological individualism nor methodological holism enables them to do justice to their subject: "It is simply arbitrary to stop at one particular stage in the explanation and say 'it is all reducible to individuals' just as much as to say it is 'all social and insti-tutional'. The key point is that in this infinite regress, neither individual nor institutional factors have legitimate explanatory primacy" (Hodgson 2004:19, see also 2010:14; Winzler 2019:434; Wrenn 2015:1232). Although the framework proposed here opens a conceptual field of pos-sibilities of social reality, nothing can be said about a concrete situation *ex ante*. This must be the subject of empirical analysis. Whether agents free themselves from handed-down institutional arrangements or co-create new ones must be reexamined for each lifeworldly situation or phenomenon. Only in this way can the claim of doing justice to a research subject be maintained, and only in this way can it be brought to light which specific institutionalisations are driven by agents and which ones are not. Not infrequently, social reality lies in the grey zones and overlap – far from the extremes that are assumed *ex ante* by methodological individualists or holists. Subjectivations and self-transfor-mations, on the one hand, and institutionalisations or institutional transforma-tions, on the other, must be respected by the researcher as possible realities in the fundamentally open processes of human interactions.

Notes

1 In developing this section, the trenchant outlines of institutionalist and pragmatist methodology by Hodgson (2003:165–66, 175), Fleetwood (2008b), Mirowski (1987) and Fuller (2013:111) were of great help.
2 This circumstance becomes especially evident at the moment when presumably 'so-cial' concepts or entities, such as 'state' or 'enterprise', are subordinated to a method-ological-individualistic logic. Cf. in this connection the immediately following third point of critique.
3 On the historical roots of this understanding of individuality in Locke, cf. Davis (2003:1.1) and Taylor (1989b).
4 Cf. the overview of heterodox economic anthropologies by Tomer (2001), some of which resist the ontologising temptation. See also Twomey (1998) with reference to Veblen's basic anthropological positions.
5 Svetlova proposes 'methodological relationism' to name a methodological position-ing that turns to this becoming as lived processes of sense-making: "If in the theory of the economic, economic activity is conceived as social sense-making and sense im-plies relational thinking, then the alternative method for economic theory is meth-odological relationism" (Svetlova 2008:140–41 see also 118, 138). There is no doubt that here, as well as with reference to the present work as a whole, there are major intersections with process philosophical thinking. See Graupe (2007), Latsis (2015), Hardt (2017), Jakobsen (2017) and Biggiero et al. (2022) on the remarkably diverse integration of process philosophy and economics.
6 This does not necessarily apply to all forms of social structures (cf. Jackson 2009:129), which is why the focus here is decidedly on the concept of institutions. Jens Beckert (2010:605), for example, introduces three forms of social structures, social networks, institutions and *cognitive frames*, whose occasional mixing or ignoring by institutional researchers he criticises. In fact, the former are ignored in the present work. With regard to the distinction between institutions and cognitive frames, however, the separation seems to be not categorical but gradual in nature, as it will be discussed later with regard to the tension between practice and reflection.

7 For economic theory, however, this means that the sharp separation of micro- and macroeconomics also belongs to the dualisms that must be overcome in the course of a reorientation of economic practice towards the phenomena and problems of the lifeworld. Individuality and sociality and their development are not phenomena that could be studied and understood separately from each other but which require an integrated analysis *in one and the same* phenomenal field (Alexander et al. 1987; cf. as example Baur 2017; Deruytter and Möller 2020).

8 Following the work of Michel Foucault (1983, 2017) an extensive research programme has emerged, particularly in sociology, that looks at the normalised patterns of becoming a subject in (post-)modern societies, and in doing so, the subject is always reflected upon as the expression of social power relations (Butler 1997; Rose 1998; Bröckling, Krasmann, and Lemke 2011). Studies such as those on the entrepreneurial self (Bröckling 2016) set out to describe dominant or at least widespread types of self-relations within certain cultural or social milieus.

   In continuation of, but at the same time critically differentiated from this strand of research, *empirical subjectivation research* has emerged in the course of the 2010s in the German-speaking context (cf. Keller, Schneider, and Viehöver 2012; Traue, Pfahl, and Globisch 2017; Geimer, Amling, and Bosančić 2018). In the image of the river metaphor, Traue et al. (2017:3) suggest that empirical subjectivation research no longer devotes itself only to the socially dominant subject positions and tacitly assumes that the subjects moving in them are carried along quasi-automatically by the current. Their concern is to approach the appropriation processes of subjectivation offers. In doing so, empirical subjectivation research not only indicates an orientation towards actors but also a stronger focus on practice – in contrast to the rather discursive and latently agentless research on subjectification of the late 20th and early 21st century (cf. Geimer and Amling 2019:24).

   Apart from the institutionalist tradition outlined here, connections to the field of economics are possible; for instance, towards the pioneering work of John B. Davis (cf. 2003:II, 2006, 2011:8–10, 2014; Davis and Marin 2009) and Amartya Sen (cf. 1985a, 1999, 2007) who, for their part, build on the concept of social identities (cf. Tajfel 1974). In fact, what could be called specifically *economic* subjectivation research has received increasing attention in recent years (Davis 2019, 2021; Hartwell 2021; Healy, Özselçuk, and Madra 2020; Mutari 2018; Ballet et al. 2018; Habermann 2008; Sen 2007, 1999).

9 Such an understanding of subjectivity bears several parallels to the social identity approaches originating in social psychology (cf. Tajfel 1974). Especially in the economic adaptations of these approaches (cf. Davis 2011:201–04); however, identity is usually negotiated as an explicit and often rigid entity. The performative production of identities in dynamic processes of subjectivation or self-transformation thus cannot be grasped.

10 Cf. for example this remark by John R. Commons: "we may define an institution as Collective Action in Control of Individual Action" (cit. as in Mirowski 1987:1026). Thelen also points to the neglect of processes of change in institutional research (2009:474):

   > Since the idea of persistence is virtually built into the definition of an institution, it should perhaps not be a surprise that the question of change is a weak spot in the literature as a whole and indeed across all varieties of institutionalism.

   Nevertheless, in recent institutional research, a stronger examination of processes of social change can be observed, which is not infrequently accompanied by an emphasis on the importance of agency (cf. Scott 2014:60; Streeck and Thelen 2005; Dolfsma and Verburg 2008; Beckert 2010; Mahoney and Thelen 2010; Unger and Smolin 2015:70; Srinivas 2020).

11 The concept of the body is preferred here to the phenomenological (and German) concept of *Leib* (Alloa et al. 2019:1; cf. Merleau-Ponty 1966:1; Waldenfels 2000) for reasons of reader-friendliness. However, following Joas (1992:3.2) and other social-scientific theories of practice (cf. Reckwitz 2003:290–91), it should not be understood in a purely material or biological way in the objectifying tradition of the Cartesian *res extensa*. The lifeworldly situated formation and transformation of the self in social processes of sense-making, running in and through all facets of the self – including the bodily ones – require an animate understanding of the body.

12 Cf. the early attempts by Irving Fisher (1926:25 ff.) to use 'utility cisterns' as allegories for stomachs for didactical reasons. Corresponding graphical representations subsequently vanish with the increasing normalisation of formalist economics, during which (graphical) plausibilisations are no longer necessary. Certainly, this postbody development had serious consequences, especially for the concept of labour as handed down from classical political economy.

13 But why the body should therefore enjoy 'primacy' in the social-scientific debate (cf. Archer 2000:106) is unclear to me. Human references to the lifeworld have more constitutive sources than just the body, whose specific meaning must be considered anew in and for each specific situation.

14 The familiarity of both experiential as well as bodily uniqueness to basic tenets of social positioning theory (cf. Lawson 2021) are obvious. The emphasis of the framework presented here lays with the relationships as opposed to the relata constituting the relationships.

15 It is precisely this individual imprint that is not accounted for in neoclassical theory, for example, but also in many heterodox schools, where, as it were, *ex ante* set individualities are predetermined, which do not allow for any differentiation, but above all, also no development.

16 Certainly, legal or constitutional concepts of freedom, which grant or assign the same freedom (from the outside) to all people, can be combined with such a conception. Here, however, the performative process indicating the lived reality of such a freedom is being highlighted.

17 The *potential* character of this human ability must be taken seriously. It is by no means said that these potentials are always and automatically used by a human being in a certain situation. In this positioning, I follow Davis in differentiation from Archer, who ontologises free action not as a possibility but in the anthropological figure of the 'active agent' (cf. Fuller 2013:120–21).

18 The same distinction can be found in Castoriadis (cf. 1997:371) between transformations of *first-order institutions* (strong) and *second-order institutions* (weak).

19 This also applies to supposedly autonomous machines, such as robots or algorithms. Institutional change, as introduced here, is a change in human reference to the lifeworld. Humans cannot exist without realising this reference, but machines can. They can be switched off by humans without ceasing to be machines.

References

Albert, Alexa, and Yngve Ramstad. 1997. 'The Social Psychological Underpinnings of Commons's Institutional Economics: The Significance of Dewey's Human Nature and Conduct'. *Journal of Economic Issues* 31(4):881–916. https://doi.org/10.1080/002 13624.1997.11505983.

Albert, Hans. 1963. 'Modell-Platonismus. Der Neoklassische Stil Des Ökonomischen Denkens in Kritischer Betrachtung'. Pp. 45–76 in *Sozialwissenschaft und Gesellschaftsgestaltung. Festschrift für Gerhard Weisser*, edited by F. Karrenberg and Hand Albert. Berlin: Duncker & Humblot.

Alexander, Jeffrey C., Bernhard Giesen, Richard Münch, and Neil J. Smelser, eds. 1987. *The Micro-Macro Link*. Berkeley: University of California Press.

Alloa, Emmanuel, Thomas Bedorf, Christian Grüny, and Tobias Nikolaus Klass, eds. 2019. *Leiblichkeit: Geschichte und Aktualität eines Konzepts*. 2nd ed. Tübingen: Mohr Siebeck.

Amariglio, Jack, and David F. Ruccio. 2001. 'From Unity to Dispersion. The Body in Modern Economic Discourse'. Pp. 143–65 in *Postmodernism, Economics and Knowledge*, edited by S. Cullenberg, J. Amariglio, and D. F. Ruccio. London; New York: Routledge.

Antony, Alexander. 2017. 'Jenseits des Dualismus zwischen "Innen" und "Außen". Eine pragmatische Perspektive auf soziale Praktiken'. Pp. 327–56 in *Pragmatismus und Theorien sozialer Praktiken: vom Nutzen einer Theoriedifferenz*, edited by H. Dietz, F. Nungesser, and A. Pettenkofer. Frankfurt: Campus Verlag.

Archer, Margaret S. 2000. *Being Human: The Problem of Agency*. Cambridge: Cambridge University Press.

Archer, Margaret S. 2003. *Structure, Agency, and the Internal Conversation*. Cambridge: Cambridge University Press.

Avtonomov, Vladimir, and Yuri Avtonomov. 2019. 'Four Methodenstreits between Behavioral and Mainstream Economics'. *Journal of Economic Methodology* 26(3):179–94. https://doi.org/10.1080/1350178X.2019.1625206.

Baggio, Guido. 2020. 'Emergence, Time and Sociality: Comparing Conceptions of Process Ontology'. *Cambridge Journal of Economics* 44(6):1365–94. https://doi.org/10.1093/cje/beaa019.

Ballet, Jérôme, Lucile Marchand, Jérôme Pelenc, and Robin Vos. 2018. 'Capabilities, Identity, Aspirations and Ecosystem Services: An Integrated Framework'. *Ecological Economics* 147:21–28. https://doi.org/10.1016/j.ecolecon.2017.12.027.

Bäuerle, Lukas. 2019. 'Optische Grenzgänge – Konstellationen Des Sehens Bei Nikolaus von Kues Und Jeremy Bentham'. *Freiburger Zeitschrift Für Philosophie Und Theologie* 66(1):92–117.

Baur, Nina. 2017. 'Prozessorientierte Mikro-Makro-Analyse. Ein Methodologischer Vergleich von Elias Und Bourdieu'. *Historical Social Research/Historische Sozialforschung* 42(4):43–74. https://doi.org/10.12759/HSR.42.2017.4.43-74.

Beckert, Jens. 2010. 'How Do Fields Change? The Interrelations of Institutions, Networks, and Cognition in the Dynamics of Markets'. *Organization Studies* 31(5):605–27. https://doi.org/10.1177/0170840610372184.

Beckert, Jens. 2016. *Imagined Futures: Fictional Expectations and Capitalist Dynamics*. Cambridge, MA: Harvard University Press.

Beckert, Jens, and Richard Bronk. 2018. 'An Introduction to Uncertain Futures'. Pp. 1–38 in *Uncertain Futures: Imaginaries, Narratives, and Calculation in the Economy*, edited by J. Beckert and R. Bronk. Oxford: Oxford University Press.

Biggiero, Lucio, Derick De Jongh, Birger P. Priddat, Josef Wieland, Adrian Zicari, and Dominik Fischer, eds. 2022. *The Relational View of Economics: A New Research Agenda for the Study of Relational Transactions*. Cham: Springer International Publishing.

Blaug, Mark. 1992. *The Methodology of Economics, or, How Economists Explain*. 2nd ed. Cambridge: Cambridge University Press.

Bögenhold, Dieter. 2020. 'History of Economic Thought as an Analytic Tool: Why Past Intellectual Ideas Must Be Acknowledged as Lighthouses for the Future'. *International Advances in Economic Research* 26(1):73–87. https://doi.org/10.1007/s11294-020-09775-3.

Bröckling, Ulrich. 2016. *The Entrepreneurial Self: Fabricating a New Type of Subject*. Los Angeles: SAGE.

Bröckling, Ulrich, Susanne Krasmann, and Thomas Lemke, eds. 2011. *Governmentality: Current Issues and Future Challenges*. New York: Routledge.

Butler, Judith. 1997. *The Psychic Life of Power: Theories in Subjection*. Stanford: Stanford University Press.

Camerer, Colin F., and George Loewenstein. 2004. 'Behavioral Economics: Past, Present, Future'. Pp. 3–52 in *Advances in Behavioral Economics*, edited by C. F. Camerer, G. Loewenstein, and M. Rabin. Princeton: Princeton University Press.

Castoriadis, Cornelius. 1997. *The Imaginary Institution of Society*. Cambridge: Polity Press.

Craib, Ian. 1992. *Anthony Giddens*. London; New York: Routledge.

Davis, John B. 2003. *The Theory of the Individual in Economics: Identity and Value*. London; New York: Routledge.

Davis, John B. 2006. 'Social Identity Strategies in Recent Economics'. *Journal of Economic Methodology* 13(3):371–90. https://doi.org/10.1080/13501780600908168.

Davis, John B. 2011. *Individuals and Identity in Economics*. Cambridge: Cambridge University Press.

Davis, John B. 2014. 'Social Capital and Social Identity: Trust and Conflict'. Pp. 98–112 in *Social Capital and Economics: Social Values, Power, and Social Identity*, edited by A. Christoforou and J. B. Davis. London; New York: Routledge.

Davis, John B. 2019. 'Explaining Changing Individual Identity: Two Examples from the Financial Crisis'. *International Journal of Pluralism and Economics Education* 10(2):208. https://doi.org/10.1504/IJPEE.2019.101726.

Davis, John B. 2021. 'The Status of the Concept of Identity in Economics'. *Forum for Social Economics* 50(1):1–9. https://doi.org/10.1080/07360932.2020.1752764.

Davis, John B., and Solange Regina Marin. 2009. 'Identity and Democracy: Linking Individual and Social Reasoning'. *Development* 52(4):500–08. https://doi.org/10.1057/dev.2009.77.

Deruytter, Laura, and Sebastian Möller. 2020. 'Cultures of Debt Management Enter City Hall'. Pp. 400–10 in *The Routledge International Handbook of Financialization*, edited by P. Mader, D. Mertens, and N. van der Zwan. London; New York: Routledge.

Dewey, John. 1939. *Theory of Valuation*. Chicago: University of Chicago Press.

Dolfsma, Wilfred, and Rudi Verburg. 2008. 'Structure, Agency and the Role of Values in Processes of Institutional Change'. *Journal of Economic Issues* 42(4):1031–54. https://doi.org/10.1080/00213624.2008.11507201.

Düppe, Till. 2009. 'The Phenomenology of Economics: Life-World, Formalism, and the Invisible Hand'. *Journal of the History of Economic Thought* 32(4):609–611.

Dupuy, Jean-Pierre. 2004. 'Intersubjectivity and Embodiment'. *Journal of Bioeconomics* 6(3):275–94. https://doi.org/10.1007/s10818-004-2926-4.

Elias, Norbert. 1998. 'Die Entstehung des homo clausus'. Pp. 173–81 in *Der Mensch als soziales Wesen: sozialpsychologisches Denken im 20. Jahrhundert*, edited by H. Keupp. München: Piper.

Fink, Eugen. 1970. *Erziehungswissenschaft Und Lebenslehre*. Freiburg i.Br.: Rombach.

Fisher, Irving. 1926. *Mathematical Investigations in the Theory of Value and Prices*. 2nd ed. New Haven: Yale University Press.

Fleetwood, Steve. 2008a. 'Institutions and Social Structures'. *Journal for the Theory of Social Behaviour* 38(3):241–65. https://doi.org/10.1111/j.1468-5914.2008.00370.x.

Fleetwood, Steve. 2008b. 'Structure, Institution, Agency, Habit, and Reflexive Deliberation'. *Journal of Institutional Economics* 4(2):183–203. https://doi.org/10.1017/S1744137408000957.

Foucault, Michel. 1983. 'The Subject and Power'. Pp. 208–28 in *Michel Foucault: Beyond Structuralism and Hermeneutics*, edited by H. L. Dreyfus and P. Rabinow. Chicago: University of Chicago Press.

Foucault, Michel. 2017. *Subjectivity and Truth: Lectures at the Collége de France, 1980–1981*, edited by F. Gros, F. Ewald, and A. Fontana. London: Palgrave Macmillan.

Friedman, Milton. 1953. 'The Methodology of Positive Economics'. Pp. 3–34 in *Essays in Positive Economics*. Chicago: University of Chicago Press.

Fullbrook, Edward. 2002. *Intersubjectivity in Economics: Agents and Structures*. London; New York: Routledge.

Fuller, Chris. 2013. 'Reflexivity, Relative Autonomy and the Embedded Individual in Economics'. *Journal of Institutional Economics* 9(1):109–29. https://doi.org/10.1017/S1744137412000239.

Geimer, Alexander, and Steffen Amling. 2019. 'Subjektivierungsforschung als rekonstruktive Sozialforschung vor dem Hintergrund der Governmentality und Cultural Studies: Eine Typologie der Relation zwischen Subjektnormen und Habitus als Verhältnisse der Spannung, Passung und Aneignung'. Pp. 19–42 in *Subjekt und Subjektivierung*, edited by A. Geimer, S. Amling, and S. Bosančić. Wiesbaden: Springer VS.

Geimer, Alexander, Steffen Amling, and Saša Bosančić, eds. 2018. *Subjekt und Subjektivierung: empirische und theoretische Perspektiven auf Subjektivierungsprozesse*. Wiesbaden: Springer VS.

Giocoli, Nicola. 2003. *Modeling Rational Agents: From Interwar Economics to Early Modern Game Theory*. Northampton: Edward Elgar.

Graupe, Silja. 2007. *The Basho of Economics: An Intercultural Analysis of the Process of Economics*. Frankfurt a.M.: Ontos.

Graupe, Silja. 2020. 'Change Is Always a Last Resort Change in Habits of Thought'. *For a New Biodiversity of Cognition in the Face of Today's Crisis* 11(3):243–54. https://doi.org/10.13140/RG.2.2.15238.19520.

Habermann, Friederike. 2008. *Der homo oeconomicus und das Andere: Hegemonie, Identität und Emanzipation*. Baden-Baden: Nomos.

Hardt, Łukasz. 2017. *Economics Without Laws: Towards a New Philosophy of Economics*. Cham: Springer International Publishing.

Hartwell, Christopher A. 2021. 'Identity and the Evolution of Institutions: Evidence from Partition and Interwar Poland'. *Forum for Social Economics* 50(1):61–82. https://doi.org/10.1080/07360932.2017.1394900.

Healy, Stephen, Ceren Özselçuk, and Yahya M. Madra. 2020. 'Framing Essay: Subjectivity in a Diverse Economy'. Pp. 389–401 in *The Handbook of Diverse Economies*. Cheltenham: Edward Elgar.

Hodgson, Geoffrey M. 1988. *Economics and Institutions: A Manifesto for a Modern Institutional Economics*. Cambridge: Polity Press.

Hodgson, Geoffrey M. 2002. 'Reconstitutive Downward Causation'. Pp. 159–80 in *Intersubjectivity in Economics: Agents and Structures*, edited by E. Fullbrook. London; New York: Routledge.

Hodgson, Geoffrey M. 2003. 'The Hidden Persuaders: Institutions and Individuals in Economic Theory'. *Cambridge Journal of Economics* 27(2):159–75. https://doi.org/10.1093/cje/27.2.159.

Hodgson, Geoffrey M. 2004. *The Evolution of Institutional Economics: Agency, Structure, and Darwinism in American Institutionalism*. London; New York: Routledge.

Hodgson, Geoffrey M. 2006. *Economics in the Shadows of Darwin and Marx: Essays on Institutional and Evolutionary Themes*. Cheltenham: Edward Elgar.

Hodgson, Geoffrey M. 2010. 'Choice, Habit and Evolution'. *Journal of Evolutionary Economics* 20(1):1–18. https://doi.org/10.1007/s00191-009-0134-z.

Hodgson, Geoffrey M. 2013. *From Pleasure Machines to Moral Communities: An Evolutionary Economics without Homo Economicus*. Chicago: University of Chicago Press.

Hollis, Martin. 1988. *The Cunning of Reason*. Cambridge: Cambridge University Press.

Jackson, William A. 1999. 'Dualism, Duality and the Complexity of Economic Institutions'. *International Journal of Social Economics* 26(4):545–58. https://doi.org/10.1108/03068299910215997.

Jackson, William A. 2009. *Economics, Culture and Social Theory*. Cheltenham: Edward Elgar.

Jaeggi, Rahel. 2018. 'Ökonomie Als Soziale Praxis'. *Zeitschrift Für Wirtschafts- Und Unternehmensethik* 19(3):343–61. https://doi.org/10.5771/1439-880X-2018-3-343.

Jakobsen, Ove. 2017. *Transformative Ecological Economics: Process Philosophy, Ideology and Utopia*. London: Routledge.

Joas, Hans. 1992. *Die Kreativität Des Handelns*. Frankfurt a.M.: Suhrkamp.

Karnøe, Peter. 1997. 'Only in Social Action!' *American Behavioral Scientist* 40(4):419–30. https://doi.org/10.1177/0002764297040004005.

Keller, Reiner, Werner Schneider, and Willy Viehöver. 2012. 'Theorie und Empirie der Subjektivierung in der Diskursforschung'. Pp. 7–20 in *Diskurs – Macht – Subjekt*, edited by R. Keller, W. Schneider, and W. Viehöver. Wiesbaden: Springer VS.

Knorr-Cetina, Karin. 1997. 'Sociality with Objects: Social Relations in Postsocial Knowledge Societies'. *Theory, Culture & Society* 14(4):1–30. https://doi.org/10.1177/026327697014004001.

Knorr-Cetina, Karin, and Urs Bruegger. 2000. 'The Market as an Object of Attachment: Exploring Postsocial Relations in Financial Markets'. *Canadian Journal of Sociology* 25(2):141. https://doi.org/10.2307/3341821.

Latsis, John. 2015. 'Shackle on Time, Uncertainty and Process'. *Cambridge Journal of Economics* 39(4):1149–65. https://doi.org/10.1093/cje/bev031.

Lawlor, Michael S. 2006. 'William James's Psychological Pragmatism: Habit, Belief and Purposive Human Behaviour'. *Cambridge Journal of Economics* 30(3):321–45. https://doi.org/10.1093/cje/bei062.

Lawson, Tony. 1987. 'The Relative/Absolute Nature of Knowledge and Economic Analysis'. *The Economic Journal* 97(388):951. https://doi.org/10.2307/2233082.

Lawson, Tony. 2021. 'Social Positioning Theory'. *Cambridge Journal of Economics*:1–39. https://doi.org/10.1093/cje/beab040.

Loasby, Brian J. 2007. 'Uncertainty, Intelligence and Imagination: George Shackle's Guide to Human Progress'. Pp. 183–97 in *The Evolution of Economic Institutions: A Critical Reader*, edited by G. M. Hodgson. Cheltenham: Edward Elgar.

Lyotard, Jean-François. 1984. *The Postmodern Condition: A Report on Knowledge*. Minneapolis: University of Minnesota Press.

Mahoney, James, and Kathleen Ann Thelen, eds. 2010. *Explaining Institutional Change: Ambiguity, Agency, and Power*. Cambridge: Cambridge University Press.

Mankiw, N. Gregory. 2021. *Principles of Economics*. 9th ed. Boston: Cengage Learning.

Mead, George Herbert. 2000. *Mind, Self, and Society: From the Standpoint of a Social Behaviorist*. 18th ed. Chicago: University of Chicago Press.

Merleau-Ponty, Maurice. 1966. *Phänomenologie der Wahrnehmung*. 1st ed. Berlin: de Gruyter.

Miller, Riel. 2018. *Transforming the Future: Anticipation in the 21st Century*. London; New York: Routledge.

Mirowski, Philip. 1987. 'The Philosophical Bases of Institutionalist Economics'. *Journal of Economic Issues* 21(3):1001–38. https://doi.org/10.1080/00213624.1987.11504695.

Mirowski, Philip. 2002. *Machine Dreams: Economics Becomes a Cyborg Science*. Cambridge: Cambridge University Press.

Mutari, Ellen. 2018. 'Metaphors, Social Practices, and Economic Life: ASE Presidential Address'. *Review of Social Economy* 76(1):1–18. https://doi.org/10.1080/00346764.2 017.1306750.

O'Sullivan, Mary A. 2021. 'History as Heresy: Unlearning the Lessons of Economic Orthodoxy'. *The Economic History Review* 75(2):297–335. https://doi.org/10.1111/ ehr.13117.

Ötsch, Walter Otto. 2019. *Mythos Markt. Mythos Neoklassik: das Elend des Marktfundamentalismus*. Marburg: Metropolis.

Reckwitz, Andreas. 2003. 'Grundelemente Einer Theorie Sozialer Praktiken/Basic Elements of a Theory of Social Practices'. *Zeitschrift Für Soziologie* 32(4):282–301. https://doi.org/10.1515/zfsoz-2003-0401.

Rose, Nikolas. 1998. *Inventing Our Selves: Psychology, Power and Personhood*. Cambridge: Cambridge University Press.

Saito, Yoshimichi. 1991. 'The Transcendental Dimension of Praxis in Husserl's Phenomenology'. *Husserl Studies* 8(1):17–31. https://doi.org/10.1007/BF00204916.

Scott, W. Richard. 2014. *Institutions and Organizations*. 4th ed. Thousand Oaks: SAGE Publications.

Sen, Amartya. 1977. 'Rational Fools: A Critique of the Behavioral Foundations of Economic Theory'. *Philosophy & Public Affairs* 6(4):317–44. www.jstor.org/ stable/2264946.

Sen, Amartya. 1985a. 'Goals, Commitment, and Identity'. *Journal of Law, Economics, & Organization* 1(2):341–55. https://doi.org/10.1093/oxfordjournals.jleo.a036895.

Sen, Amartya. 1985b. 'Well-Being, Agency and Freedom: The Dewey Lectures 1984'. *The Journal of Philosophy* 82(4):169–221.

Sen, Amartya. 1999. *Reason before Identity*. Oxford: Oxford University Press.

Sen, Amartya. 2007. *Identity and Violence: The Illusion of Destiny*. London: Penguin.

Shackle, G. L. S. 1949. *Expectations in Economics*. Cambridge: Cambridge University Press.

Spong, Heath. 2019. 'Individuality and Habits in Institutional Economics'. *Journal of Institutional Economics* 15(5):791–809. https://doi.org/10.1017/S1744137419000171.

Srinivas, Smita. 2020. 'Institutional Variety and the Future of Economics'. *Review of Evolutionary Political Economy* 1(1):13–35. https://doi.org/10.1007/s43253-020-00010-7.

Streeck, Wolfgang, and Kathleen Ann Thelen, eds. 2005. 'Introduction: Institutional Change in Advanced Political Economies'. In *Beyond Continuity: Institutional Change in Advanced Political Economies*. Oxford: Oxford University Press.

Svetlova, Ekaterina. 2008. *Sinnstiftung in der Ökonomik: wirtschaftliches Handeln aus sozialphilosophischer Sicht*. Bielefeld: transcript.

Tajfel, Henri. 1974. 'Social Identity and Intergroup Behaviour'. *Social Science Information* 13(2):65–93. https://doi.org/10.1177/053901847401300204.

Taylor, Charles. 1989a. 'Embodied Agency'. Pp. 1–22 in *Merleau-Ponty: Critical Essays*, edited by H. Pietersma. Washington, DC: University Press of America.

Taylor, Charles. 1989b. *Sources of the Self: The Making of the Modern Identity*. Cambridge, MA: Harvard University Press.

Thelen, Kathleen. 2009. 'Institutional Change in Advanced Political Economies'. *British Journal of Industrial Relations* 47(3):471–98. https://doi.org/10.1111/j.1467-8543.2009.00746.x.

Tomer, John F. 2001. 'Economic Man vs. Heterodox Men: The Concepts of Human Nature in Schools of Economic Thought'. *The Journal of Socio-Economics* 30(4):281–93. https://doi.org/10.1016/S1053-5357(01)00100-7.

Tool, Marc R. 1985. *The Discretionary Economy: A Normative Theory of Political Economy*. Boulder: Westview Press.

Traue, Boris, Lisa Pfahl, and Claudia Globisch. 2017. 'Potentiale Und Herausforderungen Einer Empirischen Subjektivierungsforschung'. In *Geschlossene Gesellschaften. Verhandlungen des 38. Kongresses der Deutschen Gesellschaft für Soziologie in Bamberg 2016*, edited by S. Lessenich. Eigenverlag DGS.

Twomey, P. 1998. 'Reviving Veblenian Economic Psychology'. *Cambridge Journal of Economics* 22(4):433–48. https://doi.org/10.1093/oxfordjournals.cje.a013727.

Unger, Roberto Mangabeira. 1987. *False Necessity: Anti-Necessitarian Social Theory in the Service of Radical Democracy*. Cambridge: Cambridge University Press.

Unger, Roberto Mangabeira. 2007. *The Self Awakened: Pragmatism Unbound*. Cambridge, MA: Harvard University Press.

Unger, Roberto Mangabeira, and Lee Smolin. 2015. *The Singular Universe and the Reality of Time: A Proposal in Natural Philosophy*. Cambridge: Cambridge University Press.

Voorberg, William H., Victor J. J. M. Bekkers, and Lars G. Tummers. 2015. 'A Systematic Review of Co-Creation and Co-Production: Embarking on the Social Innovation Journey'. *Public Management Review* 17(9):1333–57. https://doi.org/10.1080/14719037.2014.930505.

Waldenfels, Bernhard. 1997. *Topographie Des Fremden. Studien Zur Phänomenologie Des Fremden 1*. Frankfurt a.M.: Suhrkamp.

Waldenfels, Bernhard. 2000. *Das Leibliche Selbst: Vorlesungen Zur Phänomenologie Des Leibes*. edited by R. Giuliani. Frankfurt a.M.: Suhrkamp.

Weick, Karl E. 1979. *The Social Psychology of Organizing*. New York: McGraw-Hill.

Winzler, Tim. 2019. 'The Superiority of Economics and the Economics of Externalism – A Sketch'. *Science in Context* 32(4):431–47. https://doi.org/10.1017/S0269889720000058.

Wrenn, Mary V. 2015. 'Agency and Neoliberalism'. *Cambridge Journal of Economics* 39(5):1231–43. https://doi.org/10.1093/cje/beu047.

Zilber, Tammar B. 2002. 'Institutionalization as an Interplay between Actions, Meanings, and Actors'. *The Academy of Management Journal* 45(1):234–54. https://doi.org/https://doi.org/10.5465/3069294.

Zucker, Lynne G. 1977. 'The Role of Institutionalization in Cultural Persistence'. *American Sociological Review* 42(5):726. https://doi.org/10.2307/2094862.

4 Praxis, reflection and the vertical gap

In the previous two sections, I first introduced the human relationship to the lifeworld by means of socially shared sense-making procedures. Then, with the concept of institutional agency, a social field of tension of this process was opened, as well as a conceptual framework for the question of 'who' actually (re)produces social imaginaries. In the following section, this horizontal field of tension will be expanded by including another field of tension: the 'how' – i.e., the *modus operandi* of sense-making processes. The section will identify a vertical gap, which, in order to approach, we will first name the two poles between which the gap exists. Schütz introduces two essential modes of sense-making:

> Our daily life . . . is a permanent oscillating between contemplative and practical attitudes, between interpreting the surrounding world and practical reaction to it, between deliberating and planning and the execution of these plans. And in great crises of our lives, we sit down and analyse our problems as objectively and theoretically as possible. 'We stop and think', as Dewey put it.
>
> (Schütz 1996:43)

On the one hand, our everyday dealings with the lifeworld have an *executive* character. We act in reference to what presents itself to us as lifeworld. I will introduce the concept of (social) *praxis* for this mode in a moment. On the other hand, what Schütz calls contemplation opens up a mode of human sense-making that has to be sharply separated. People can decide to interrupt the supposedly thoughtless process and let it become the object of reflection. This objectification of the performative process in reflection always has profound effects on agents and the social process they carry out. They change the primarily practical relationship to the world into a more strongly reflected or 'theoretical' one.[1] Human sense-making oscillates between these two extremes, in most empirical cases probably manifesting itself in the overlapping areas. These can be classified according to the degree of reflection of lived practice and will now be stratified in an ideal-type manner. Before introducing a respective model, however, practice as the primordial (i.e., original) mode of

DOI: 10.4324/9781003371687-4

human existence in the world and the refractions and dynamics associated with the mode of reflection should first be briefly elaborated upon.

Praxis

In Chapter 2 human existence was introduced as a relational one, insofar as it inevitably always refers to a tangible lifeworld. At the same time, it was interpreted as a processual, unfinished one, insofar as the meaningful references to the lifeworld are always in a state of continuous change. It is precisely these fundamental aspects of human existence that can be captured by the concept of *praxis*:

> The Greek word <praxis> (πράξις [π.]) and all the secondary forms belonging to it go back etymologically to περα (beyond, further, longer). From a diminutive by-form πρα-, πρήσσω/ πράττω (Ionic: I pass through or Attic: I execute, perform, do) has arisen by κ-extension.
>
> (Kleger 2019:1278; my translation)

The Greek term praxis, as is shown by its secondary forms, is a referential term: praxis always *refers* to a reality (πράξη) that exists only in the singular. This reality was introduced here as the lifeworld. Praxis, hence, means an experience (πείρα) or a procedure (πρακτική) with and within this reality. Praxis can thus be interpreted as an active reference to the lifeworld; it is the *modus operandi* of human sense-making. Human praxis, as is implied, is at the same time the form of existence that precedes all other possible references to the lifeworld. Human life is "primordially practical" (Hua XV, 328). Nothing can be realised by human beings 'outside' of praxis; all human references to the lifeworld are praxis. This comprehensive aspect is already indicated by the Greek root of the concept of praxis:

> '*theoria* is one of the best forms of *praxis*' [EN: Aristotle, *Pol.* 1325b 21 f., *Eth. Nic.* 1177a 20]. Therefore, it may not be too much to say that Aristotle did not have the strict distinction between 'theory' and 'practice' in the modern sense.
>
> (cf. Depraz 2000:97; Saito 1991:18)

Contemplation, however abstract and supposedly withdrawn, turns out to be a form of praxis: "Even a practice that denies its 'practical character' remains a practice. . . . The 'context of incoherence' is still a context" (Jaeggi 2018:359; my translation).[2] If one connects these thoughts on the concept of praxis with what was introduced in the preceding section, it could be consistently extended to the concept of *social practice* and, at the same time, specified in the tradition of social science theories of practice (cf. Reckwitz 2003). References to the lifeworld are then always *both* practical *and* social in the sense that they build on collective routines and knowledge, reproduce or innovate them *in actu*. According to such an understanding, actions are

> embedded . . . in a broader, socially shared practice held together by an implicit, methodological and interpretative knowledge as a typified, routinised and socially 'understandable' bundle of activities. The social here . . . is to be sought in the collectivity of behaviours [held] together by a specific 'practical skill'.
>
> (Reckwitz 2003:289; my translation)

Far from being individualistic excesses of the mind, sense-making is thus a collective process that is always performatively situated in the lifeworld and thus always bears a *material* side; it is tangible and can be approached (for instance, for scientific endeavours).

Reflection

If human existence is fundamentally practical, how can social phenomena be examined and differentiated at all? The very ability to formulate this question presupposes the human capability that is now to be examined. People not only continuously create meaning in relation to the lifeworld but can also make their sense-making practice the object of reflection. As the term already suggests, reflection implies something being reflected, thrown back. This means no more (but also no less) than that people can make their own action - even if it is a reflexive one - the object of thought. In these reflexive practices, something new is brought forth – either as content of reflection or as the very act of carrying out the reflection. This creativity of reflective practice means that the thoughts gained in reflection, the language developed and the images produced can never keep pace with practice. Reflection, *as reflection*, is always late. The fundamental difference between praxis and reflection and the dynamics of human reference established by this difference is what I call the vertical gap (cf. Figure 4.1).

The central concept of institutional agency also proves useful in the context of the vertical axis because it indicates praxis as an inescapable *modus operandi* of human references to the lifeworld (. . . *agency*) and, at the same time, refers to more or less reflected systems of rules that limit the spectrum of potential practices (*institutional* . . .). The vertical axis, as was established in the previous section with reference to theories of practice, intersects with the tensions on the horizontal axis. Regardless of the degree of their reflection, practices are always also social - even when the genius withdraws and creates radical innovations: "Just as there is no private language, there is no private practice" (Svetlova 2008:110; see also Jaeggi 2018:347–48).[3] Nevertheless, as the following remarks will show, the potentials for social enforcement of social practices increase towards the middle of the scheme.

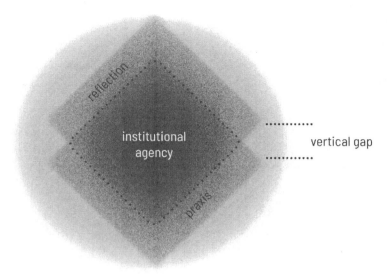

Figure 4.1 Fundamental difference between reflection and practice in the *modus operandi* of human references to the lifeworld

Reflection – like all forms of praxis – can take on a wide variety of forms or medialities. In Western intellectual history, language is the most frequently thematised medium with the help of which relationships towards the self and the world are being reflected upon. Methodologically, this circumstance is expressed, for example, in a pronounced discourse or narrative research (cf. Morgan and Wise 2017), which can also be found with reference to narrative processes of sense-making in economic matters (cf. Klamer, McCloskey, and Solow 1989; Maeße 2013; McCloskey 1998; Roos and Reccius 2021). The decisive point here is that narratives are not 'added' to 'genuinely' economic phenomena, as Shiller (2019) suggests, but that 'the economic' *is* the narrative creation of meaning (along with other forms of sense-making). Within such an understanding, 'economic' practices and entities are those that can be designated as such in social resonance (cf. Chapter 5).

Research on imagination, but also artistic research, shows that the mediality of reflections is more diverse than the spoken or written word. However, language or images are only ever a medium and not a guarantor of reflection. As, for instance, critical marketing research (cf. Tadajewski and Maclaran 2009: chapter II) shows, images and language can be used precisely in such a way that they prevent reflection. In this case, practices do not become the object of thinking but of a forced language- or image-mediated habituation. In the elaboration of the following model of action, I recommend always keeping these different medial qualities in mind.

A new model for action

The conception of reflection *as practice* makes it impossible to dissolve human sense-making into 'pure practice' on the one hand and 'pure reflection' on the other, which are then placed in an abstract relationship *ex post*. Through the overlapping of reflection and practice, a continuum of human modes of sense-making emerges, the primary distinguishing feature of which is reflective intensity: How strongly is a practice shaped by reflection (cf. Figure 4.2)?

By stratifying different levels of reflection, models of human forms of practice can be formed, the simplest of which in economics is probably the behavioural science dichotomy of System 1 and System 2 (cf. Kahneman 2013:1). The following proposal is meant to contribute to respective literature in institutional economics, where these distinctions are of particular relevance. The

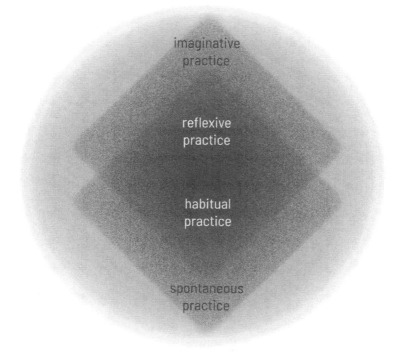

Figure 4.2 Different forms of practice, stratified by degree of reflection

model differentiates between four different levels in the field of tension between praxis and reflection, and in doing so, also offers a way of highlighting further drivers of institutional transformation that complement those already identified in the preceding section. The sharp separation of the different forms of practice is certainly an ideal one, which in itself does not do justice to lived practices. The model is not intended to depict but to open up a space for reflection, with the help of which lived practices of sense-making can be better understood. It thus joins an emerging field of research in German-speaking areas that undertakes a practice-theoretical foundation to economic thinking (cf. Svetlova 2008; Beckert 2016; Hochmann 2016; Jaeggi 2018; Knobbe 2021).

Spontaneous practice

In the spectrum of different degrees of reflected practice, spontaneous practice appears at the 'least' or 'not at all' reflected end. This form of practice was already called *performance of spontaneity* early on: "As long as we live naively along in the vivid presence of our stream of thought our life is a totality of possible performances of spontaneity" (Schütz 1996:43–44). Spontaneous practice has no meaning apart from itself, as its meaning lies in the practice itself. It refers to something outside itself (the lifeworld), and this active reference is simultaneously the source of meaning. The division of ends and means is not compatible with this form of practice. It is to be distinguished, for example, from the concept of production, which finds its root in the Greek *poiesis* and, depending on the degree of reflection, would have to be assigned to one of the other three following forms of practice. A production always has a purpose apart from it. It takes place on the basis of a plan determined *before* production (*causa formalis*) or for a purpose that determines it but lies outside the production process itself (*causa finalis*). This distinction has profound implications, especially for a possible understanding of economic action in the sense of a spontaneous practice:

> When conceiving the economical as *praxis*, activities are carried out that 'pursue no end . . . and leave no result outside themselves . . . whose full meaning is rather exhausted in the accomplishment itself . . . the accomplishment is the effected or the work . . . not an objectively tangible produced thing, but only the activity in its actuality. This actuality of its own lies beyond the end-means category.' [H. Arendt: Vita activa, 1960 kohlhammer, p. 201].
>
> (Svetlova 2008:190, cf. also 2008:130, 189)

Because of its radical executional character, which does not (yet) know a separation of ends and means and has not (yet) been broken and interpreted by reflection, this form of practice is a pre-conscious and pre-individual one. Its mode is a genuinely social one, insofar as its relatedness to the lifeworld always implies a relatedness to other people (see also Jaeggi 2018:347–48; cf. Svetlova 2008:110). Spontaneous practice precedes self-consciousness and makes the latter possible in the first place: "our continuous sense of self, or self-consciousness, emerges from our practical activity in the world" (Archer 2000:3). In spontaneous practice, Cartesian dualisms are overcome insofar as it, as Hodgson emphasises with reference to Joas, contains a strong bodily facet that is by no means opposed to a *res cogitans* but makes such a *res* possible in the first place (cf. Hodgson 2010:12; cf. the same argumentation with reference to the phenomenological tradition in Depraz 2000:106; see also Archer 2000:26). Even if self-consciousness in spontaneous practice plays a subordinate role in this reading, this process is only realised in and through the activities of actual living people. In this respect, spontaneous practice may be pre-egological, but certainly not un-human or super-human. As with social institutions, which cannot be realised without actual living people, so it is also with practice (cf. Reckwitz 2003:292).

Although many, perhaps the large part, of our everyday actions are of a routinised or planned nature, it is an inescapable quality of human performances that they are never completely absorbed in plans or habits. Human action understood in this way is not accompanied or projected by reflections but simply realised by people in the here and now. Spontaneous practice is a thoroughly *present* form of practice that is neither determined by a specific imprint of the past (habitual practice) nor by future-oriented planning (reflective practice) or a seemingly timeless imagining (imaginative practice).

In its quality as indeterminately productive, spontaneous practice is, at the same time, identified as a potential source of institutional transformation. Performance in a strict sense – i.e., pre-reflective action – can bring forward new forms of relating to the world that were previously unknown. As soon as such a new practice has been realised, it is 'in the world' and thus already an innovation in itself. Furthermore, it can give rise to social imitation; thus, to the beginning of institutionalisation or to reflexive confrontation. Spontaneous practice can emerge from both the individual and the social pole; the performative, brief abandonment of learned social routines or formed intentions can be produced by individuals and by social groups (cf. Svetlova 2008:106). The circles that such a realisation of spontaneous potentiality draw can be far-reaching and, in extreme cases, even trigger a profound institutional transformation. In any case, its origin is an empty one, insofar as the new was not intended and does not spring from a plan, but only *provokes* intentionality and rational penetration. Hans Joas calls the creative quality of the performative a "meaningful loss of intentionality" (cit. as in Svetlova 2008:102).

Another illustration of spontaneous potentiality can be found in the iteration as described by Derrida: "it is also by virtue of this reiteration that gaps and fissures are opened up as the constitutive instabilities in such constructions, as that which escapes or exceeds the norm, as that which cannot be wholly defined or fixed by the repetitive labour of that norm" (Butler 1993:10).

Iterations are continuous repetitions of institutionalised relations, which, however, are minimally changed at the same time with each repetition. Svetlova (cf. 2016:193) illustrates this point by referring to the example of a play that is presented differently with each repetition and never in complete accordance with the script. It is what has already been described in institutionalism as *discreteness* (cf. Tool 1985; Streeck and Thelen 2005:7–8, 19).

Habitual practice

The next form of practice, already saturated with a certain quality of reflection, is now introduced with the term *habitual practice*. In the literature on institutional economics, the concept of *habit* has enjoyed a central position from the very beginning (Hodgson 2004:14, cf. 2010:4, 6–7). Habits of thought and action are thus at the core of the concept of institutions; indeed, one could say that institutions are realised and carried forward above all in habitual practice (cf. Hodgson 2003:164). The concept of habit refers to a learned and highly routinised practice that is characterised by a regularity due to this routinisation. This regularity has repeatedly led social scientists to confuse habits with necessities or even laws of action (cf. Panther 2020:461). Habits, however, are not of a necessary nature but gain their stability through unquestioned practice in social resonance. Habits have, as John Dewey (cf. 1922:42) and also Bourdieu (cf. 2013:72, 82) formulate it, a 'dispositive' character. Their continuation is probable but not necessary.[4] At the same time, previously learned but subsequently neglected habits can be taken up again. This always depends on the lifeworldly conditions that agents encounter in another of the forms of practice formulated here.[5]

Crucially, habitual practice is more reflexive in character than spontaneous practice. However, the reflection is of a concealed or implicit nature. Habits are carried out on the basis of implicit knowledge, which is precisely why they are so powerful. This specific quality of 'habitual knowledge' has already been described by various authors as 'tacit knowledge' (Michael Polanyi), 'conjunctive knowledge' (Karl Mannheim), 'practical consciousness' (Anthony Giddens) or 'logic of practice' (Pierre Bourdieu) (cf. also Beckert 2003:774). It allows for a largely smooth, collective practice amongst agents who share the same implicit knowledge. For example, visitors to a supermarket in present day Spain know that they can only enter during opening hours, that they can take a shopping trolley with them to transport the goods, that they should not dance or shout loudly in the supermarket, that they are not allowed to eat or destroy the goods in the supermarket itself, that they have to queue to buy the goods at the checkout and then pay there, etc. This knowledge must be shared when visiting the supermarket. Yet, it does not have to be read up on or studied when visiting the supermarket. Agents who have learned it simply 'have' it and they are therefore able to navigate the context of the vast majority of supermarkets without breaking the implicit rules. And it is precisely because everyone shares this knowledge that the social reality called 'supermarket' can emerge and – under the condition of further material and immaterial institutions – be continuously maintained. At the same time, the supermarket example points to the ways in which agents form habitual knowledge. They learn it in the lived participation in social contexts where this knowledge applies.[6] Even if newcomers to a social context may initially be irritated by the habits that apply there, regular participation in these contexts will quickly lead to the acquisition of the respective habitual knowledge (cf. Fleetwood 2008a:251). In this respect, habitual knowledge is not learned from textbooks or from manuals. In quite a few cases, such as the supermarket, it does not have to be verbalised or even written down. This is especially evident in those moments when new habits must be formed. For example, in order to introduce the new rule of wearing masks during the coronavirus pandemic, numerous symbols were established and written or verbal admonitions were given to reconfigure the social reality called 'supermarket'. A change in social habits often requires explicit communication, whereas the retention of habits does not.

The temporality typical of the formation and realisation of habitual practice is thus primarily determined by the past. Habitual practice usually continues practices learned in the past; it is practice driven by memory (cf. Schütz 1996:26). In the mode of habitual practice, the past is handed down in the present towards the future. Although often pre- or non-linguistically, this habitual knowledge inherent in social practices can be explicated or reconstructed. Quite a few methods of qualitative social research have specialised in precisely this endeavour (cf. Chapter 6).

Reflexive practice

If we move up one level in the model of different forms of practice developed here, we arrive at reflexive practice. This is the area that has been called intentional or wilful action. One of the most prominent theorists of this form of practice is Alfred Schütz (1932), who conceived his theory of the meaningful construction of the social world as a theory of planned, reflexive action. Here, the practical reference to the lifeworld is divided into two phases. First, an action is designed which is then, in a sense, carried out (cf. Svetlova 2008:29). We have already introduced the distinction between *praxis* and *poiesis* above. While the meaning of spontaneous praxis is absorbed in its execution (and is thus not of a divided or sequential nature), the meaning of production (*poiesis*) lies in the product to be produced. It is precisely this separate notion of sense-making, in which meaning is first created and then subsequently 'lived out', that lies at the core of Schütz's concept of action, which he also uses synonymously with the concept of work because of its poietic character (cf. Schütz 1996:30).

A practice set up in this way no longer bears natural, but consciously planned features. It is not implicit but explicit knowledge that guides and drives this form of practice. And, insofar as this knowledge is actively negotiated or possibly even generated by the reflexive agent, reflexive practice can also be described as an act of will: "The capacity to change both behaviour and goals without external stimulus means that humans have a *will*" (Hodgson 1988:11; see also Schütz 1996:30). People can formulate an explicit will for themselves or together,[7] which is then implemented. The temporality of this form of practice is thus future-oriented. It develops images or plans of a future practice and, in this openness to the creation of a new reality, also holds strong transformational potential. Here, practice is not determined by the past but can be redefined. Thus, future-oriented, reflexive practice is close to the idea that in principle the future can be planned.

One of the most important forms reflexive practices can take is language. In mutual or self-conversation, agents develop plans, weigh things up and finally decide what to do. But pictorial sketches, diagrams or graphical instructions can also form such planned knowledge. In the medium of the image, they show without words, but explicitly, what is to be done. Another form of this knowledge can be seen in mathematical knowledge and calculation. Agents - for example, planning authorities or managers of companies - rationalise their possible courses of action in mathematical form. According to formally prescribed rules and constraints, they calculate an action to be realised. For the academic examination of this reflexive practice, it is crucial not to lose sight of its interpretative character and its lifeworldly situatedness. *These* specific agents use *there* and *then* a mathematically composed knowledge to deal with the lifeworld.[8]

At this point, the reader may already have asked about the origin of the plans to be realised. How and where do plans for reflexive practice arise? As already hinted at, one possibility comes from planning or anticipating actions. In these instances, present action is directed towards (i.e., reflected by) imagined futures (Beckert 2016).[9] At the same time, however, it also points to a second temporality of reflexive practice. In addition to the future-oriented reflexive practice, there is also a second, past-oriented reading. Here, the reflection of one or more agents is not directed towards a practice to be carried out but towards a practice that has already been realised. What have we done? How did it go? Am I satisfied with the result? Here, practice does not become a *project*, but an *object* of reflection. This simultaneously addresses a cross-connection to other forms of practice: spontaneous or habitual or imaginative practices can become the object of reflection. This is precisely the endeavour of reconstructive social research. With the help of abductive methodologies, previously implicit knowledges are made explicit (cf. Chapter 6). In this way, new knowledge about a now-reflected practice emerges. But even non-scientific reflections can reveal new, unexpected aspects that were unanticipated in this way in the retrospective of every act, no matter how meticulously planned. Reflected past practice can then enter the planning process of future (reflected) practice as now-explicit knowledge. This is where the productive (poietic) character of reflective practice becomes apparent. In the sequential layering of planning, executing, reflecting, planning, executing, etc., new options for action emerge. Both types of reflexive practice share a harboured sequential – i.e., divided – time structure. Whether the reflection is directed towards the practice before or after, it never coincides with it (Schütz 1996:43–44). In this difference between the realisation and the reflection of the realisation, nothing else is revealed than the *vertical gap* already introduced. We have seen above that praxis can never be caught up reflexively. In the context of reflective practice, this gap is now elevated to a virtue, so to speak, or even used as a resource; we can plan practice or we can learn from past practice. In this sense, reflective practice is not present- (like spontaneous practice) but always future- or past-oriented and, compared to habitual practice, more sequential.

However, the realisation of plans need not coincide with what is planned, no matter how well thought out in advance. Then the tension of the vertical gap becomes apparent *in actu*. This experience (as a disappointed expectation) can, in turn, become the object of reflection and lead to the adjustment of plans. Nevertheless – and this is its paradox – reflective practice (like any other form of practice) always has an executional side as well (cf. endnote 2): it reflects in the present. Even if the objects of reflexive practice lie in the future or the past (however small the 'distance'), it is always present *as praxis*.

With reference to the phenomenological tradition, when introducing the human capability to reflect, it is important to emphasise that only with its help can reflected identities and explicit self-images be produced – which, however, at the same time demand the price of distancing oneself from oneself as an agent: "reflection is made possible by the primary distance which arises from the incessant flow of the self-distantiation prior to reflection" (Saito 1991:27). In spontaneous practice, we simply *do* without asking the question of who we are or become in the process. It is different from the moment when reflections come into play. As Saito (1991:21) emphasises with reference to Husserl, every reflective act always implies a self-transformation. The reflecting agent becomes another one in the process of reflection. This process of change becomes particularly clear when she herself is both the reflecting agent *and* the object of reflection. In this process of self-assurance, the self achieves the paradox of producing another version of itself while maintaining this self in the constant repetition of this process. The paradox of establishing a reflected identity thus lies in the fact that it can only ever achieved at the price of performative self-sacrifice. Self-assurance is always preceded by self-distancing, however marginal.[10] As we shall see, this distancing in the vertical gap is thus also an essential driving force of institutional transformation.

Imaginative practice[11]

Schütz had introduced a triumvirate of contemplative practices in distinction to intentional action: dreaming, theorising and imagining. The latter will now be elaborated here as a fourth form of practice.[12] He introduces imaginative practice as *creative contemplation*. The peculiar tension of imaginative practices stems from an interesting imbalance. On the one hand, there is a pronounced reflexivity, which is why it is placed at the top of the model. Nevertheless, it is inherent in this activity that it refers neither to past nor to future practices. Schütz goes so far as to say that it does not have to refer to the everyday world at all and, in this respect, may be considered timeless. Instead of encountering this everyday world with a 'full awakeness' or 'attentiveness' (cf. Schütz 1996:39), agents reflexively (not performatively!) withdraw into an imaginative sphere in the mode of an imaginative practice:

> Although imagining may be projected, it always lacks the intention to realise the project; that is, it lacks the purposive 'fiat'. . . . Although I am not acting when imagining a performance of spontaneity, I may imagine myself as acting and even working. Thus, the imagined acting may refer to a project, it may have its in-order-to and because motives, it may originate in choice and decision. Even more, it may show intentions to be realised and it may be fancied to be gearing into the outer world. However, all this belongs to the imageries produced by the imagining, etc. Imagining itself is necessarily inefficient and remains outside the hierarchies of plans and purposes that are valid in the world of working. The imagining self does not transform the outer world.
>
> (Schütz 1996:39)

Imaginative practice does not pursue goals or purposes, as it lacks the *pragma* (Lat.: the affair, the course of business). This is precisely why it is the reflexive counterpart to spontaneous practice. Imagining has a strong executional character that does not, however, turn towards the lifeworld but away from it. While spontaneous practice is always directed (impartially) towards the lifeworld and opens up new potentials in it, imagination is directed towards nothing and can draw something new from this void. At the same time, this peculiar reference to nothing makes it possible to develop imaginations that must appear completely unreal on the basis of the established institutions of thought and action: "the imaginary ultimately stems from the original faculty of positing or presenting oneself with things and relations that do not exist" (Castoriadis 1997:127). The unfamiliar and sometimes absurd is an essential characteristic of what imaginers generate. The reality of the imagination offers its own possibilities that do not (have to) apply in lifeworldly practices. The temporality and spatiality of imagining as a practice situated in the lifeworld can be overcome in the imagined (cf. Schütz 1996:40). However, this should not obscure the fact that imaginative practice, as a bodily-bound and spatio-temporally situated practice, is still a practice 'happening' in the lifeworld.

Its fundamental openness grants imaginative practice to be the potential source of radically new relationships towards the lifeworld. This creative potential is used in phenomenologically inspired social research (cf. Castoriadis 1997; Gurwitsch 1979) but also in the field of institutional research (cf. Unger 2007; Beckert 2011:24; Panther 2020). It cannot be planned; the imagining would be poietic in nature and one would only re-encounter the planned. Nevertheless, imagining can give rise to imaginations and simulations, or it can lead to plans and projections. While spontaneous practice has no problem of realisation (because, once enacted, it is always already 'in the world'), the imagined – if intended – must first be transformed from potentiality into reality (cf. Urpelainen 2011:216). Strictly speaking, the imagined is initially 'only' an 'unenacted institution' (Urpelainen 2011:224) which then *can* be realised in lifeworldly events, if they are brought into connection with established institutions (cf. Castoriadis 1997:127).

However, as Castoriadis points out, established social imaginaries are also entangled with imaginative practice in another way. They form part of the fabric' of imaginations. The fact that something can be newly connected or that a new image is created at all is also made possible by the fund of images already available. In this context, Schütz (cf. 1996:37) emphasises the role of art as a possible source of inspiration for imaginative practice (see also Greene 2007). Paintings, music, performing arts, etc., can stimulate a generation of new patterns of meaning. However, this is not a genuine quality of art. It can also – like other forms of expression – directly undermine creative potential if, for example, images are set in a way that they appear to have no alternative. The medium of the image can also be used for manipulative purposes and end up as imaginary prisons.

This addresses the less charming side of imaginative practice, which shows itself in its incessant consummation – but without being connected to other forms of practice, and especially not to the lifeworld. Put more simply: Imaginative practice can also provoke an imaginative loss of the lifeworld (which, in principle, cannot be achieved performatively). In the imaginative retreat from lifeworldly dependencies lies the potential for bringing forth the new, but at the same time the danger of losing that to which the new could refer: the lifeworld. In this context, standard economics, standing in a model-platonic tradition (cf. Albert 1963), can be regarded as a powerful example of imaginative practice. Quite a few of its methodological conventions are based on a forced retreat from the world, which was undertaken in the hope of finding certainties, if not truths, in the imaginaries of the calculating mind. Even if the 'frozen imaginaries' gained this way do not have a resonant relationship to the tangible lifeworld, they can nevertheless shape the latter to a very strong degree if they enter into shared social practices and are perpetuated there, for example, in a habitual reproduction (cf. endnote 11). Indeed, the transformation of powerful imaginaries such as those of the 'objective scientist', 'the market' or 'the utility maximiser' into social habits of thought and action can be considered an essential moment of contemporary economic education (Bäuerle 2020, 2021).

One last important point should be made in this context with Schütz: "Imagining may occur lonely or socially" (Schütz 1996:40). This sentence contains the paradox that imaginations are realised in socially shared medialities. Successful imaginative communication, for example, is necessarily dependent on the rules of language usage, but within these rules, it unfolds an imaginative practice that goes beyond or extends these rules. New images and new languages are developed in the process of speaking, which then exist as images or words but by no means have to conform to the possibilities and limits of the lifeworld. Here, too, the paradoxical character that imaginative practices can assume becomes apparent.

Overlapping and interactions

Now that four essential forms that practice can take have been introduced, the supposedly hard boundaries between them are to be dissolved again immediately. For a comprehensive understanding of lived social reality, it is vital to address the possible overlaps and interactions between different forms of practice. Schütz will once again be the inspiration for this endeavour:

> daily life in the world is not <occurring> on one single level of reality. During a single day or even a few hours we run through several levels. Performing our daily duties, we do not live exclusively in that tension of consciousness that we called 'full-awakeness'. To the contrary, our consciousness shows a permanent oscillation among all possible degrees of tension; it runs through the whole gamut of *attention à la vie*.
> (Schütz 1996:43)

Schütz emphasises that we pass through several modes of practice in our everyday lives and that lived social processes can never be resolved to one of the poles of the tension between practice and reflection. Rather, he describes the mode of individual or social references to the lifeworld as a continuous oscillation between those poles, without needing the vacillation to be a constant object of volitional decisions. Even the simple example of (reflexive) planning, the successful execution of which always requires the habitual use of language or thought, shows that human practice does not take place in the either-or, but rather in simultaneous layering. We encounter this simultaneity of different forms of practice again and in a heightened notion in the social dimension. In one and the same board meeting of a company, spontaneous, habitual, reflexive and imaginative practices of the agents involved may overlap at one moment.

Social scientific practice must take into account this fact of the possible plurality of forms of practice as well as the unpredictability of social reality induced by it. Just as the relationship between individuality and sociality in a concrete social phenomenon can never be determined *ex ante*, the specific forms of practice through which this phenomenon is produced can also never be known *ex ante.* Here, too, it is important to avoid plausible but no-less-counterfactual assumptions. Hodgson, for example, criticises a one-sided setting in favour of reflexive practices within the framework of neoclassical and Austrian theoretical approaches (cf. Hodgson 1988:106 see also 58, 125).[13] And Hodgson, for his part, has also already been criticised for using a holistic notion of habit, thus undermining reflexive forms of practice (as well as possible other forms of practice, such as the two additional ones introduced here, cf. Fuller 2013:113). Such presuppositions – whether justified or not – should be avoided in favour of an open, empirical examination of the phenomenon in question. The scientific examination of a social phenomenon should therefore always assume that a variety of forms of practice is possible and only answer the question of which concrete form is revealed in empirical research (cf. Chapter 6).

In fact, 16 ideal-type interactions are possible through the forms of practice introduced here alone (cf. Figure 4.3). In the context of this book, the abundance of mutual influences of forms of practice cannot and should not be dealt with exhaustively in theory. For cursory illustration, a brief example will be explained here.

It is conceivable that a new, imagined social relationship (imaginative practice) – e.g., the figure of the 'prosumer', which transcends the classic division of production and consumption – is first captured in language or even in a drafted theory (reflexive practice), which then guides a practice through its implementation; for example, in the context of a community-based farming project, which, over time, becomes a habitual practice. If new members join who have not experienced the implementation phase and have not otherwise dealt with the role of the prosumer, they get to know and enact its routines in a social context as a matter of course. The habits stemming from the imagination may then be spontaneously broken here and there in spontaneous practice

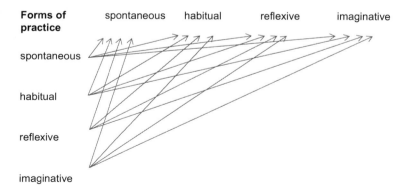

Figure 4.3 Ideal-type interactions of different forms of practice

in the field, which can undermine the established institutional relations and give rise to new ones. Instead of letting the rule-breaking become a habit directly, it is first talked about in the group (reflexive practice), the institutional structure is communicatively overhauled and subsequently translated into new practices to be habitualised, which in turn, do not have to fully comply with the linguistically or legally fixed set of rules (spontaneous practice). For its part, the explicit discussion of rules occurs on the basis of routinised patterns of action, such as language, but also the physical reference of the discussants. In the example, these patterns are not also changed by the communication about the rule-breaking.

This simple example of a both temporarily and spatially very limited economic practice underlines that an economic phenomenon can be subject to constant change in terms of the interrelated practices (re)producing it. In the tradition of institutional economics alone, many approaches are available that take as their subject matter some of these interactions and thus offer ways to do scientific justice to the diversity of real-world economic practice (cf. Fleetwood 2008b:191–92). Where these relations are hypostatised into ontologised entities, they can still at least be read and understood as *possibilities* of social practice, even without this hypostatisation.

The interactions most frequently addressed in the literature are those between what I have introduced here as reflexive practice, on the one hand, and habitual practice, on the other.[14] Fuller (cf. 2013:123–24), for example, develops an internal differentiation of different 'capabilities of the mind'. The distinguishing feature of these is the *object* of the reflections. In doing so, he also elaborates those reflections that can refer to habitual practices and even to the knowledge ('habitual beliefs') on which these practices are based (see also Spong 2019:11). For Fuller, reflections can objectify habits of thought and action and, in the (reflexive) availability thus gained, also change them in the direction of other reflected habits. A similar approach can be found in Marc Blyth's (2002) theory of institutional change. In his theory, Blyth emphasises the role of ideas in changing institutional structures. He uses the term 'institutional change' synonymously with "the *deliberate* replacement of one set of economic institutions with another" (Blyth 2002:45; my accentuation). It becomes clear that Blyth attributes the decisive power to realise institutional change to the deliberate, reflexive practices of agents. And Marc Tool (cf. 1985:75) also locates the origin of (habituated) institutions and their change in reflexive practices. Any other origins of institutional change, such as imagining or spontaneous practice, are implicitly excluded in these formulations. As a final example of the direction of impact of reflections on action, the debate surrounding the performativity of economics should be mentioned here (cf. MacKenzie, Muniesa, and Siu 2007; Boldyrev and Svetlova 2016). Performativity is not usually understood here in the spontaneous sense as introduced above but in the sense of a habitual practice. With reference to various fields ranging from central banking to supermarket facilities, the research programme elaborates how theories and mostly discursive practices of economists are able to shape the habitual practices of monetary policymakers and consumers (and not the other way around): "Economics often seems abstract (to some of its proponents, as well as to its critics), yet it also articulates with, influences, is deployed in, and restructures concrete economies in all their messy materiality and their complex sociality" (MacKenzie et al. 2007:2). The opposite direction of effect from habitual practice to reflexive practice is emphasised by Hodgson:

> reasons and beliefs themselves depend upon habits of thought. Habits act as necessary filters of experience and the foundations of intuition and interpretation. They are the grounding of both reflective and non-reflective behaviour. This does not make belief, reason or will any less important or real.
>
> (Hodgson 2010:6; see also Lawlor 2006)

Reflection and communication, according to Hodgson, always take place on the basis of habitual patterns. The latter therefore have a significant influence on and limit reflexive practice. Hodgson also explicitly discusses this facet of the question of subjectivation – i.e., the processes of creating a sense of self. The formation of explicit identities, for example, is always based on habitual patterns of self-signification (cf. Hodgson 2002:170). Archer, for her part, goes one step further by attributing to spontaneous practices the possible effect of influencing or laying the foundations for habits, even to the point of reflected identity norms (cf. Archer 2000:7–8, 134). The connections between the extremes of imaginative and spontaneous practice are certainly an extraordinary case in the true sense of the word. These processes can be imagined as experimental explorations in which performative and imaginative free spaces are opened up and filled in ever new iterations and thus a successive establishment of new institutional patterns coming to life.

These examples show that the interactions between different forms of practice can be extremely diverse if they are not subjected in advance to an ontologising regularity. Understanding these interactions and thus deciphering the *specific mode* of producing social reality is a difficult task for the social sciences because it is linked to the tension between agency and social structures, as introduced before. From an institutionalist point of view, all introduced forms of practice offer possibilities for overcoming or successively transforming established institutions. In this context, the aforementioned peculiarities of the vertical gap show that, while the potentialities undoubtedly increase at the margins (i.e., at the very top or bottom), *the potentiality of their realisation*, as it were, decreases. At the core of the model, and especially in the area of habitual practice, the greatest degrees of institutionalisation are found (graphically indicated by an increasing colour intensity in the centre). Softening or even changing these with the help of spontaneous or imaginative potentials is a difficult undertaking because they have to be asserted against established institutions. Institutional research interested in institutional transformation can never sufficiently focus only on potentialities but must always also address the performative preconditions for their realisation.

Before assessing the methodological prerequisites for social and economic science to enter into adequate epistemic relationships with these realities, the outlined framework shall now be bend towards the central question of what 'the economy' actually is.

Notes

1 In fact, the distinction introduced here with reference to phenomenology can be traced back to the Aristotelian conceptual pair *'praxis'* and *'theoria'* (cf. Bernstein 1971:xiii ff.). Husserl's analogous terms would be *Strömen* and *Zeitigung* (cf. Hua XV, 350).

2 This also means that all forms of practice to be introduced later always bear the performative character of the concept of practice established here. Such a primacy of practice is also shared by institutional economists but is often limited to *a specific form of practice* through its identification with the concept of habit (cf. Hodgson 2002:171, 2003:166, 2010:6). This restriction is not shared here through a differentiation of different forms of practice.

3 It is precisely at this point that Ludwig von Mises' so-called 'praxeology' falls short. It must contend with three fundamental problems: firstly, it is radically individualistic, insofar as all motives for action arise from the individual; "thinking is always a manifestation of individuals" (von Mises 1998:178; my translation). In this respect, it has to do with the problems of methodological individualism previously discussed. Furthermore, he thinks of these motives exclusively at the level of what will later be introduced as reflective practice. Motives are explicit in nature; individuals are aware of them. Thus, within the framework of von Mises' praxeology, it is not possible to map other forms of practice, let alone operationalise them empirically. Third, the place and time of economic practices remain fundamentally indeterminate due to Mises' aggressive anti-historicism. In von Mises' thinking, practice is not a historical process, but the result of an imagined decision-making behaviour in a simulated world with 'precisely determined preconditions': "The theory of action differs from nomothetic empirical science in that its propositions, as propositions of an a priori theory, claim unexceptional validity under the precisely determined preconditions. It is strict science" (von Mises 1940:43; my translation). And further: "The praxeological concepts are exact and can be applied with full exactness to reality. But this reality is always the reality of action, not the reality as it presents itself to the scientific observation of the external world. Insofar as praxeology considers the things of the external world, it considers them in terms of their relation to human unsatisfactoriness" (von Mises 1940:63; my translation). Thus, von Mises' 'praxeology' is not suitable for the study of situated practices in the lifeworld but, at best, of imagined practices in imagined environments – prominently in that of 'The Market'.

4 In this respect, habits also differ from instincts. As Hodgson (cf. 2003:167, 2010:8) emphasises, instincts cannot be changed in social processes. This means, however, that they cannot be conceptualised as social imaginaries in relation to a tangible lifeworld. Instincts are not 'transmitted' in the medium of social meaning but in biological and thus pre-social dispositions. That is why they are not part of the outlined framework.

5 Here, Hodgson draws the difference between the concept of habit and the concept of behaviour:

> Habit does not mean behaviour. It is a propensity to behave in particular ways in a particular class of situations. Crucially, we may have habits that lie unused for a long time. A habit may exist even if it is not manifest in behaviour. Habits are

submerged repertoires of potential behaviour; they can be triggered by an appropriate stimulus or context. . . . Because some habits can be triggered by conscious resolve, they are not the same as the behaviourist stimulus-response mechanism or conditioned reflex.

(Hodgson 2003:164)

In this reading, the central concept of the behavioural sciences offers even less potential for change than that of habits, especially if one wants to grant the behaving agents the possibility of changing their behaviour in a self-determined way (and not only induced from the outside) (see the same interpretation in Schütz 1996:27). Homer Simpson and Mr. Spock (cf. Thaler and Sunstein 2008:22) are the misleading ends of a short-falling spectrum. Since the concept of habit opens up a greater bridge to the other forms of practice introduced here, it is preferred to the concept of behaviour.

6 The example of the sciences shows very clearly that this proposition does not only apply to supposedly everyday, pre-reflexive or habitual practice but also in those very social settings that are characterised by a great deal of reflexivity and explicit knowledge. The social reality called 'science' and its inherent practices are also based on implicit habitual knowledge of the agents involved. The investigations of Mannheim (1964), Fleck (1980), Kuhn (1996) and Bourdieu (1988), amongst others, can be regarded as foundational works in this respect. Corresponding reflections with reference to the economic sciences can be found, for instance, in McCloskey (1994), Boldyrev and Svetlova (2016) and Bäuerle, Pühringer, and Ötsch (2020).

7 This is precisely where methodological individualists would disagree. They see no possibility of people forming a collective, shared will through communication and then realising it. Actions always arise only from individual plans or preferences. Davis (2003:133–34) proposes the terms 'group intention', 'collective intention' or 'we-intention' for collective wills. Cf. also Searle (1995:1) and Tuomela and Miller (1988).

8 The *Social studies of economics* (cf. Maeße et al. 2021; MacKenzie, Muniesa, and Siu 2007; Boldyrev and Svetlova 2016) impressively demonstrate that quite a few of these calculative lifeworldly practices stem from the economic sciences themselves. These findings remind us of the fact that 'the economy' and economic science are always (re)produced in one and the same reality.

The question, however, of how, for instance, a *homo economicus* makes choices in his own abstract sphere must necessarily remain meaningless because it lacks any empirical reality in the sense introduced here: an imagined *homo economicus* does not relate to the lifeworld in a meaningful way; he realises the operations assigned to him by the imagining scientist (cf. Svetlova 2008:40–41). Therefore, standard economic modelling falls under what is introduced below as imaginative practice (cf. Shackle 1992:1). Epistemologically, we are dealing with an imaginative form of scientificity. Within this imaginative framework, economics enacts rationalising techniques.

9 The futures economic agents envision, according to Beckert, can be brought into life by all forms of practice as outlined in this chapter (cf. endnote 11). Hence, there are also 'imagined' futures developed by means of reflexive practices; for instance, in the form of a business plan or a political decision based on forecasting.

10 This does not apply to identities carried on in the modus of habitual practice. Here, due to the implicit, largely unreflected status of identities, self-conceptions bear a thoroughly hardened quality. Identity politics heavily rely on the perpetuation and exploitation of such hardened conceptions of self and/or of communities. As the outlined framework indicates, such processes can be broken anytime by changing the *modus operandi* of producing social reality; hence, its reflexive intensity.

11 In the following explanations, 'imagination' is to be understood strictly as practice in the sense of 'imagining'. Imaginations or *imaginaries* in the medial – i.e., in the representational – sense are to be sharply distinguished from this: "we have to sharply

distinguish between imagining as a performance of spontaneity and the imagined imageries" (Schütz 1996:39). Such images (of the self, of society, of the future, of strangers, etc.) naturally also play an important role in other forms of practice, such as habitual or reflexive ones. "Imagined futures" (cf. Beckert 2016), for example, can be (re)produced within all forms of practice examined here. 'To imagine' in the sense introduced here, on the other hand, means a specific form of practice.

12 The concept of dreaming is introduced by Schütz as a decidedly individual one: "the monad with all its mirroring of the universe is indeed without windows when it dreams" (Schütz 1996:43). This raises doubts as to whether dreaming *understood in this way* can be the subject of social science research. Especially since it still does not represent a reference to the lifeworld in the sense introduced above (the reference would be the practice of sleeping). If one were to abandon the individualistic criterion (for example, through the fact that dreams are reflected upon *after dreaming* and are thus transferred into social medialities), one would gain a concept of dreams that would come very close to Schütz's concept of imagination.

With regard to the peculiarities of theorising, Schütz does not seem to introduce a categorial difference to imagining, but rather, a difference of the social agents carrying the action (the former being carried out by scientists). In concentrating on the conceptual qualities of imaginative practice, I leave such a distinction aside that leads me to characterise some forms and examples of scientific research as imaginative practice. Indeed, mainstream economics can be reflected upon as a powerful example of a tradition largely relying on imaginative practices.

13 In the causal terminology of Fleetwood (2008b:189–90) the same problem of the two authors prominently cited here, Archer and Hodgson, becomes apparent: "Whereas for Archer, the chain of causality runs from reasons, through reflexive deliberations to intentions, for Hodgson the chain of causality has a prior stage, rooted instincts, and habits".

14 This is partly due to the fact that these two forms of practice dominate the literature in institutional economics. Imaginative and spontaneous forms of practice also form marginal areas in this field.

References

Albert, Hans. 1963. 'Modell-Platonismus. Der Neoklassische Stil Des Ökonomischen Denkens in Kritischer Betrachtung'. Pp. 45–76 in *Sozialwissenschaft und Gesellschaftsgestaltung. Festschrift für Gerhard Weisser*, edited by F. Karrenberg and Hand Albert. Berlin: Duncker & Humblot.

Archer, Margaret S. 2000. *Being Human: The Problem of Agency.* Cambridge: Cambridge University Press.

Bäuerle, Lukas. 2020. 'Reproduction, Deconstruction, Imagination. On Three Possible Modi Operandi of Economic Education'. *JSSE – Journal of Social Science Education* 19(3):21–36. https://doi.org/10.4119/JSSE-3378.

Bäuerle, Lukas. 2021. 'The Power of Economics Textbooks. Shaping Meaning and Identity'. In *Power and Influence of Economists: Contributions to the Social Studies of Economics*, edited by J. Maesse, S. Pühringer, T. Rossier, and P. Benz. London; New York: Routledge.

Bäuerle, Lukas, Stephan Pühringer, and Walter Otto Ötsch. 2020. *Wirtschaft(Lich) Studieren. Erfahrungsräume von Studierenden Der Wirtschaftswissenschaften.* Wiesbaden: Springer VS.

Beckert, Jens. 2003. 'Economic Sociology and Embeddedness: How Shall We Conceptualize Economic Action?'. *Journal of Economic Issues* 37(3):769–87. https://doi.org/ https://doi.org/10.1080/00213624.2003.11506613.

Beckert, Jens. 2011. 'Imagined Futures. Fictionality in Economic Action'. *MPIfG Discussion Paper* 11(8).

Beckert, Jens. 2016. *Imagined Futures: Fictional Expectations and Capitalist Dynamics.* Cambridge, MA: Harvard University Press.

Bernstein, Richard J. 1971. *Praxis and Action: Contemporary Philosophies of Human Activity.* Philadelphia: University of Pennsylvania Press.

Blyth, Mark. 2002. *Great Transformations: Economic Ideas and Institutional Change in the Twentieth Century.* New York: Cambridge University Press.

Boldyrev, Ivan, and Ekaterina Svetlova, eds. 2016. *Enacting Dismal Science: New Perspectives on the Performativity of Economics.* New York: Palgrave Macmillan.

Bourdieu, Pierre. 1988. *Homo Academicus.* Frankfurt a.M.: Suhrkamp.

Bourdieu, Pierre. 2013. *Outline of a Theory of Practice.* 28th ed. Cambridge: Cambridge University Press.

Butler, Judith. 1993. *Bodies That Matter: On the Discursive Limits of 'Sex'.* London; New York: Routledge.

Castoriadis, Cornelius. 1997. *The Imaginary Institution of Society.* Cambridge: Polity Press.

Davis, John B. 2003. *The Theory of the Individual in Economics: Identity and Value.* London; New York: Routledge.

Depraz, Natalie. 2000. 'The Phenomenological Reduction as Praxis'. Pp. 95–110 in *The View from Within: First-Person Approaches to the Study of Consciousness,* edited by J. Shear and F. J. Varela. Thorverton: Imprint Academic.

Dewey, John. 1922. *Human Nature and Conduct: An Introduction to Social Psychology.* New York: Henry Holt and Company.

Fleck, Ludwig. 1980. *Entstehung Und Entwicklung Einer Wissenschaftlichen Tatsache.* Frankfurt a.M.: Suhrkamp.

Fleetwood, Steve. 2008a. 'Institutions and Social Structures'. *Journal for the Theory of Social Behaviour* 38(3):241–65. https://doi.org/10.1111/j.1468-5914.2008.00370.x.

Fleetwood, Steve. 2008b. 'Structure, Institution, Agency, Habit, and Reflexive Deliberation'. *Journal of Institutional Economics* 4(2):183–203. https://doi.org/10.1017/S1744137408000957.

Fuller, Chris. 2013. 'Reflexivity, Relative Autonomy and the Embedded Individual in Economics'. *Journal of Institutional Economics* 9(1):109–29. https://doi.org/10.1017/S1744137412000239.

Greene, Maxine. 2007. *Releasing the Imagination: Essays on Education, the Arts, and Social Change.* Princeton: Jossey-Bass.

Gurwitsch, Aron. 1979. *Phenomenology and the Theory of Science.* Evanston: Northwestern U.P.

Hochmann, Lars. 2016. *Die Aufhebung der Leblosigkeit: eine praxis- und naturtheoretische Dekonstruktion des Unternehmerischen.* Marburg: Metropolis.

Hodgson, Geoffrey M. 1988. *Economics and Institutions: A Manifesto for a Modern Institutional Economics.* Cambridge: Polity Press.

Hodgson, Geoffrey M. 2002. 'Reconstitutive Downward Causation'. Pp. 159–80 in *Intersubjectivity in Economics: Agents and Structures,* edited by E. Fullbrook. London; New York: Routledge.

Hodgson, Geoffrey M. 2003. 'The Hidden Persuaders: Institutions and Individuals in Economic Theory'. *Cambridge Journal of Economics* 27(2):159–75. https://doi.org/10.1093/cje/27.2.159.

Hodgson, Geoffrey M. 2004. *The Evolution of Institutional Economics: Agency, Structure, and Darwinism in American Institutionalism.* London; New York: Routledge.

Hodgson, Geoffrey M. 2010. 'Choice, Habit and Evolution'. *Journal of Evolutionary Economics* 20(1):1–18. https://doi.org/10.1007/s00191-009-0134-z.

Jaeggi, Rahel. 2018. 'Ökonomie Als Soziale Praxis'. *Zeitschrift Für Wirtschafts- Und Unternehmensethik* 19(3):343–61. https://doi.org/10.5771/1439-880X-2018-3-343.

Kahneman, Daniel. 2013. *Thinking, Fast and Slow*. New York: Farrar, Straus and Giroux.

Klamer, Arjo, Deirdre N. McCloskey, and Robert M. Solow. 1989. *The Consequences of Economic Rhetoric*. Cambridge: Cambridge University Press.

Kleger, Heinz. 2019. 'Praxis, Praktisch'. Pp. 1277–307 in *Historisches Wörterbuch der Philosophie, Band 7, P-Q*. Darmstadt: Wissenschaftliche Buchgesellschaft.

Knobbe, Sonja. 2021. *Ökonomische Praktiken: zur theoretischen Fundierung eines alltäglichen Begriffs*. Baden-Baden: Nomos.

Kuhn, Thomas S. 1996. *The Structure of Scientific Revolutions*. 3rd ed. Chicago: University of Chicago Press.

Lawlor, Michael S. 2006. 'William James's Psychological Pragmatism: Habit, Belief and Purposive Human Behaviour'. *Cambridge Journal of Economics* 30(3):321–45. https://doi.org/10.1093/cje/bei062.

MacKenzie, Donald A., Fabian Muniesa, and Lucia Siu, eds. 2007. *Do Economists Make Markets?: On the Performativity of Economics*. Princeton: Princeton University Press.

Maeße, Jens. 2013. 'Das Feld und der Diskus der Ökonomie'. Pp. 241–75 in *Ökonomie, Diskurs, Regierung*, edited by J. Maeße. Wiesbaden: Springer VS.

Maeße, Jens, Stephan Pühringer, Thierry Rossier, and Pierre Benz, eds. 2021. *Power and Influence of Economists: Contributions to the Social Studies of Economics*. London; New York: Routledge.

Mannheim, Karl. 1964. *Wissenssoziologie*. Berlin: Hermann Luchterhand.

McCloskey, Deirdre N. 1994. *Knowledge and Persuasion in Economics*. Cambridge: Cambridge University Press.

McCloskey, Deirdre N. 1998. *The Rhetoric of Economics*. 2nd ed. Madison: University of Wisconsin Press.

Morgan, Mary S., and M. Norton Wise. 2017. 'Narrative Science and Narrative Knowing. Introduction to Special Issue on Narrative Science'. *Studies in History and Philosophy of Science Part A* 62:1–5. https://doi.org/10.1016/j.shpsa.2017.03.005.

Panther, Stephan. 2020. 'Imagination Und Institution. Ein Essay'. Pp. 445–66 in *Jenseits der Konventionen: Alternatives Denken zu Wirtschaft, Gesellschaft und Politik: Eine Festschrift für Walter O. Ötsch, Kritische Studien zu Markt und Gesellschaft*. Marburg: Metropolis.

Reckwitz, Andreas. 2003. 'Grundelemente Einer Theorie Sozialer Praktiken/Basic Elements of a Theory of Social Practices'. *Zeitschrift Für Soziologie* 32(4):282–301. https://doi.org/10.1515/zfsoz-2003-0401.

Roos, Michael W. M., and Matthias Reccius. 2021. 'Narratives in Economics'. *Ruhr Economic Papers* 922.

Saito, Yoshimichi. 1991. 'The Transcendental Dimension of Praxis in Husserl's Phenomenology'. *Husserl Studies* 8(1):17–31. https://doi.org/10.1007/BF00204916.

Schütz, Alfred. 1932. *Der Sinnhafte Aufbau Der Sozialen Welt*. Wien: Julius Springer.

Schütz, Alfred. 1996. *Collected Papers Volume IV*. The Hague: Martinus Nijhoff.

Searle, John R. 1995. *The Construction of Social Reality*. New York: Free Press.

Shackle, G. L. S. 1992. *Epistemics & Economics: A Critique of Economic Doctrines*. New Brunswick: Transaction Publishers.

Shiller, Robert J. 2019. *Narrative Economics: How Stories Go Viral and Drive Major Economic Events*. Princeton: Princeton University Press.

Spong, Heath. 2019. 'Individuality and Habits in Institutional Economics'. *Journal of Institutional Economics* 15(5):791–809. https://doi.org/10.1017/S1744137419000171.

Streeck, Wolfgang, and Kathleen Ann Thelen, eds. 2005. 'Introduction: Institutional Change in Advanced Political Economies'. In *Beyond Continuity: Institutional Change in Advanced Political Economies*. Oxford: Oxford University Press.

Svetlova, Ekaterina. 2008. *Sinnstiftung in der Ökonomik: wirtschaftliches Handeln aus sozialphilosophischer Sicht*. Bielefeld: transcript.

Svetlova, Ekaterina. 2016. 'Performativity and Emergence of Institutions'. Pp. 183–200 in *Enacting Dismal Science: New Perspectives on the Performativity of Economics, Perspectives from Social Economics*, edited by I. Boldyrev and E. Svetlova. New York: Palgrave Macmillan.

Tadajewski, Mark, and Pauline Maclaran, eds. 2009. *Critical Marketing Studies*. London: SAGE Publications.

Thaler, Richard H., and Cass R. Sunstein, eds. 2008. *Nudge: Improving Decisions about Health, Wealth, and Happiness*. New Haven: Yale University Press.

Tool, Marc R. 1985. *The Discretionary Economy: A Normative Theory of Political Economy*. Boulder: Westview Press.

Tuomela, Raimo, and Kaarlo Miller. 1988. 'We-Intentions'. *Philosophical Studies* 53(3):367–89. https://doi.org/10.1007/BF00353512.

Unger, Roberto Mangabeira. 2007. *Free Trade Reimagined: The World Division of Labor and the Method of Economics*. Princeton: Princeton University Press.

Urpelainen, Johannes. 2011. 'The Origins of Social Institutions'. *Journal of Theoretical Politics* 23(2):215–40. https://doi.org/10.1177/0951629811400473.

von Mises, Ludwig. 1940. *Nationalökonomie. Theorie Des Handelns Und Wirtschaftens*. Genf: Editions Union.

von Mises, Ludwig. 1998. *Human Action: A Treatise on Economics*. Scholar's edition. Auburn: Ludwig von Mises Institute.

5 What is the economy? An interim conclusion

Barely five minutes of TV news, five paper presentations at a random scientific conference or five pages of fiction or non-fiction bestsellers pass by without 'the economy' being mentioned. In fact, talk (in the name) of 'the economy' might be seen as a defining signature of life in economised times and societies: "This policy is good or bad for the economy", "Representatives of the economy demand more federal support", "2022 is expected to be a better year for the economy". Moreover, we experience an ever-exploding inflation of 'economies': the informational economy, the platform economy, the purpose economy, the social market economy, the digital economy, the green economy, etc. At first sight, the prominence of the concept and its multiple usages might cause one to expect a heightened awareness – at least in academia – of the meaning(s) of 'the economy' in contemporary societies. Yet, on further inspection, I am inclined to state that, reflexively, 'the economy' remains a barely touched (research) topic, just as Godin, Gaglio, and Vinck (2021:2) formulate it with regard to the term 'innovation':

> As a concept that travels easily between social spheres and between scientific disciplines and as a concept that is programmatic and performative (Godin and Gaglio 2019), innovation remains a relatively unstudied concept. To be sure, studies by the hundreds are published every year on innovation. But this literature studies innovation as a fact or reality, without considering discursive and conceptual issues. What use is made of the concept, for what purposes, by whom, are questions that remain unstudied, with a very few exceptions.

This is why I deem it most useful, maybe even necessary, to penetrate economic talk with the simple yet most difficult question of what the economy actually is. This chapter is not meant as a final answer but as an invitation to invigorate public, inclusive discussions about the question of actual and possible economies.

In the relationship to a lifeworld that cannot be overcome over a lifetime, people develop and pass on social imaginaries in order to deal with this very

DOI: 10.4324/9781003371687-5

lifeworld in social resonance. From these more or less reflected sense-making processes, (re)produced in everyday practices, social institutions arise. Economic processes can be understood as a subset of human references to the lifeworld; namely, those called 'economic'. There is no absolute understanding or universal definition of what an economy or 'the economic(al)' is. The meaning of 'the economy' does not derive from abstract rules or definitions but from ongoing social practices of sense-making: "What makes meaning meaningful is not its particular function within statements (as in Kant), but it lies in the achievement of sense (*Sinnvollzug*), that is, in the act of carrying out" (Düppe 2009:24; Ötsch 2019:8; see also Schmidt-Wellenburg and Lebaron 2018:1). To make a long story very short: the economy is what we, together, call the economy.

Thus, 'the economy' is nothing more (and nothing less!) than that which is signified as such in a collective act of sense-making: "That is why sense-making, instead of utility maximisation, is declared to be the central principle, and sense a key concept in the *theory of the economic*" (Svetlova 2008:133, see also 2016:191). In their economic actions, agents not only (re)produce a material sphere but also social imaginaries in which these actions appear to be meaningful. Meaning is, so to speak, both a prerequisite and a by-product of every economic action. The lifeworld is not simply a given for economic agents (for example, in its constitution as a space of goods with expectable quanta of utility), nor is its reflexive or performative relatedness set *ex ante* (for example, in the form of preference orders and utility functions). In every situation, agents experience the lifeworld yet again and relate to it in ways unknown *ex ante*.

To conceive 'the economy' as such an "instituted process" (McGregor and Pouw 2016:1129 ff.) implies a firm rebuke of naturalistic accounts of the economy, stating that the economy is guided by a set of (hidden) laws or mechanisms that economists or other scientists can set out to uncover. In a strict sense, the economy *is* not something, but it is *becoming* something. To illustrate this point on a discursive level, it means that a term like 'the economy' – like any other term – is arbitrary. It is empty, to frame it negatively; it is open, to frame it positively. Hence, there is no absolute, ever-true or substantial core of 'the' economy. Rather, this imagined core consists of an active, socially shared performance that relies on traditions and handed-down rules – but is always open to potential change. Hence, what is being negotiated as 'the economy' essentially depends both on the specific narratives and imaginaries as well as the tangible phenomena (the people, the spaces, the artifacts, etc.) that are connected with them. Certainly, the former plays the decisive role, since their limits decide what may be perceived as an economic phenomenon – and what may not. What has been known to linguistics for over a century as the phenomenon of *linguistic relativity* (cf. Swoyer 2015) or *arbitrariness* (cf. Schwarz 2019) has gained rising attention in the discipline's mainstream lately (cf. Chen 2013; Shiller 2019). In heterodox economics (cf. Klamer, McCloskey, and Solow 1989; McCloskey 1998) as well as in other social sciences (Maeße 2013; Schmidt-Wellenburg and Lebaron 2018), an extensive tradition analyses the discursive contents, conjunctures and production processes of 'the economy'. Recent developments in economic sociology (Beckert 2016; Beckert and Bronk 2019), socioeconomics (Ötsch and Graupe 2018, 2020), Cultural Studies (Du Gay and Pryke 2002; Ray and Sayer 1999) and Political Economy (Levy and Spicer 2013; Sum and Jessop 2013) point to the imaginative landscapes in which 'the economy' unfolds – in central economic realms such as consumption, money and credit and, obviously, socio-technological innovation. In part, these research approaches advance beyond the medium of language and investigate the pictorial representations of 'the economy'.

A first example arises when conceptualising entrepreneurial practices as sense-making endeavours that produce – depending on the realised meaning – different social or entrepreneurial realities (cf. Weick 1995; Svetlova 2010; Dekker, Remic, and Dalla Chiesa 2020). Actually, the mere naming of a corporation can already be regarded as an act of entrepreneurial sense-making which must be realised again and again so that – amongst other preconditions – a corporation may persist as such (cf. Searle 2010:98). What kind of 'economy' is being handed down if 'entrepreneurship' or 'corporations' are framed in this or that way? What are the motivations to found and run an enterprise (social, sustainable, profitable, etc., entrepreneurships)? How is the enterprise linked to the wider social, cultural and/or natural environments? Which actions, artefacts, groups and languages are perceived and debated as 'typical' entrepreneurial entities at all? Answering these questions will reveal all too different forms of entrepreneurships and, along with it, a different understanding of 'the economy'.

Another powerful example of a specific meaning of 'the economy' can be gained from the history of economics. Kenneth Boulding, for instance, defined "the econosphere as that subset of the sociosphere, or the sphere of all human activity, relationships, and institutions, which is particularly characterized by the phenomenon of exchange [measured in terms of money; L.B.]" (Boulding 1966:2). To frame only those phenomena that are driven by exchange calculated in terms of money as 'economical' is most certainly possible – but is by no means necessary. For Boulding, and possibly his students and related scholars (maybe even dissenters of an emerging mainstream!), this definition allowed him to investigate 'the economy' with respective methods suitable to approach processes and institutions of money-based exchange. But one has to keep in mind that the reason why he was able to do so was an arbitrary decision in the first place, that could have gone in completely different directions. And one could go through the history of this specific conception of 'the economy', studying its ideational origins and developments, its institutional impact, and so on, and then contrast the history of this specific conception with another one circulating in human history and ask questions such as "Why was it, that this concept survived and the other did not?". The point I am focussing on here is that any concept connected with 'the economy' is any closer to an imagined 'truth' or 'core' of 'the' economical – but that we are looking on a more or less heated battleground of the signification of the economy (cf. Figure 5.1).

A third example might be drawn from one of the most prominent feminist critiques of standard-economic reasoning: in mainstream economics, 'the economy' is typically reduced to monetarised goods and services, their respective institutions (i.e., national accounting systems) and (predominantly male) agents (Waring 1988). Policies, public debate and remunerations are directed towards these pecuniarily codified parts of the economy. Under such imaginative preconditions, unpaid labour as mostly carried out by women is silently excluded from 'the economy', although in some national or even regional cases, the annual hours of unpaid work exceeds the paid ones (International Labour Organization 2018:56). More so, the monetarised (part of the) economy is existentially dependent on the non-monetarised (part of the) economy: careers depend on carers. Whether these epistemic shortfalls are countered by tallying different indicators (i.e., hours worked) or whether counting itself is an expression of patriarchal structures in modern societies to be overcome is subject to ongoing debate in feminist economics and beyond (Tejani 2019). In any case, the discussion will frame a different economy.

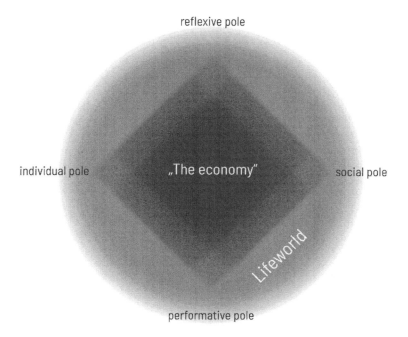

Figure 5.1 'The economy' as a battleground of meaning between four poles

The examples show that totally different economies emerge by means of definitory power and respective techniques, as institutionalised, for instance, in national accounting systems. What economy would emerge from an hours-worked-centred perspective? What economy would arise from its understanding as those practices in society contributing to the well-being of actual living people without harming ecological boundaries or social foundations? What economy is embedded in the 17 SDG goals? What would it mean to regulate 'the economy' in these cases, respectively? What topics would emerge from these possible significations that, so far, remain neglected in public, parliamentary, organisational or private debates on 'the economy'? What would amount to something beneficial – or detrimental – for 'the economy'? Who should be invited as a talk show guest as a representative of 'the economy'?

In a praxeological context, it has to be pointed out, once again, that the question of what is being perceived as 'the economy' is not just talk or a purely academic question. The interpretative framework we collectively connect with the term has substantial consequences on the design and redesign of economic life – of livelihoods. When, for instance, the general public and political decision-makers frame 'the economy' as a process to be measured in produced monetary wealth (GDP) and/or unemployment rates, it is the respective figures alone that count and that potential political action is directed to. The tangible phenomena *before* or *beside* these figures – working conditions, unpaid labour, ecological impact, etc. – are implicitly delegated to the realm of the non-existent or non-important in 'economic' matters. Actually, all sorts of phenomena that could also be interpreted in quantitative or qualitative terms as 'the economy' are implicitly neglected. The acts of rendering certain possible meanings unnecessary or even inexistent have been described in critical epistemologies as tendencies of epistemic injustice (Fricker 2007) or epistemic violence (Brunner 2020). Having lost or never seen the public limelight, alternative concepts and the specific realities they address cannot inspire a directed development or transformation of social institutions. Hence, the imaginary abandonment of certain (possible or actual) economies may yield far-reaching impact on the everyday lives of people. As the powerful example of discourses on care work show, the neglected realities may play a decisive role in terms of lived practices and significance for a smooth functioning of the 'mainstream economy'. Yet, since the institutionalised narrative and imaginative framework does not measure 'the economy' in terms of hours worked but in terms of revenue made, these realities are not perceived as 'the economy'. In sum, the question of 'What is the economy?' is an utterly normative one; it raises the question of power in collective processes of sense-making (Maesse 2021). Who is actually having a say? Who is able to contribute to a naming and actual framing of 'the economy' in terms of interpretative content?

While economists working in the tradition of Boulding, for instance, certainly have proficiency in dealing with 'economic' matters in the specific frame outlined by Boulding, there is no and never will be an absolute justification of this or any other frame in the first place. Hence, what is needed for any concept of the economy (whether originating from science or not) is a second-order justification of the fundamental frame laying beneath the entire tradition. Why is it that we – as a nation, as a group, as a city, as a generation – should proceed with your concept of the economy? Some will put forward a conservative argument: we should proceed with our term because it is what science has brought about. Some will put forward a pragmatist argument: we should proceed with our term because it will help solve a real-world issue at hand. The point is that, while the internal criteria of any such justification may be driven in rigor to the extremes (first-order legitimations), there is no absolute standpoint capable of justifying any second-order legitimation for any specific scheme of interpretation (of the economy). The justification of these different notions is and will always remain a political process, and hence, relies on values or norms fostered within a community.

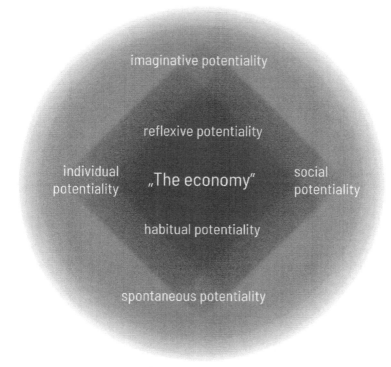

Figure 5.2 'The economy' as emerging from six different potentialities of institutional transformation

In sum, 'the economy' is that signified as such. Such processes of sense-making arise from the fundamental relationship of people in need of inter-preting the lifeworld. The emptiness of 'the economy' is not a deficit of a segregated or even unscientific debate – it is just the display of the funda-mental openness of economic relationships, practices and institutions. Yes, the economy is an endless 'discovery procedure' (Hayek 1993:67) – but this procedure also applies to what living people mean by the term 'the econ-omy'. Its predominant link to 'The Market' or 'competition' is not the end of the debate but one possibility next to endless different possibilities to frame the economy – and, to be most clear, to frame what we mean by the term 'market'. The tradition of economics itself (www.exploring-economics.org), neighbouring social sciences but also public culture (Lash and Urry 1994) referring to 'the economy', have brought about a deep plurality of possible economic meanings (cf. Figure 5.2). Working with these potentials construc-tively can lead to all sorts of economic practices and institutions – to all sorts of real-world economies (cf. Gibson and Dombroski 2020). The contribution to and fostering of a public and scientifically informed debate about eco-nomic possibilities, their dangers and advantages, will be an important task for professional economists having revitalised this fundamental openness of 'the economy'.

References

Beckert, Jens. 2016. *Imagined Futures: Fictional Expectations and Capitalist Dynamics*. Cambridge, MA: Harvard University Press.

Beckert, Jens, and Richard Bronk. 2019. 'Uncertain Futures: Imaginaries, Narratives, and Calculative Technologies'. *MPIfG Discussion Paper* 19(10).

Boulding, Kenneth. 1966. 'The Economics of Knowledge and the Knowledge of Economics'. *The American Economic Review* 56(1/2):1–13.

Brunner, Claudia. 2020. *Epistemische Gewalt: Wissen Und Herrschaft in Der Kolonialen Moderne*. Bielefeld: transcript.

Chen, M. Keith. 2013. 'The Effect of Language on Economic Behavior: Evidence from Savings Rates, Health Behaviors, and Retirement Assets'. *American Economic Review* 103(2):690–731. https://doi.org/10.1257/aer.103.2.690.

Dekker, Erwin, Blaž Remic, and Carolina Dalla Chiesa. 2020. 'Incentives Matter, But What Do They Mean? Understanding the Meaning of Market Coordination'. *Review of Political Economy* 32(2):163–79. https://doi.org/10.1080/09538259.2019.1628341.

Du Gay, Paul, and Michael Pryke. 2002. 'Cultural Economy: An Introduction'. Pp. 1–20 in *Cultural Economy: Cultural Analysis and Commercial Life, Culture, Representation, and Identities*, edited by P. Du Gay and M. Pryke. London; Thousand Oaks: SAGE.

Düppe, Till. 2009. 'The Phenomenology of Economics: Life-World, Formalism, and the Invisible Hand'. *Journal of the History of Economic Thought* 32(4):609–611.

Fricker, Miranda. 2007. *Epistemic Injustice: Power and the Ethics of Knowing*. Oxford; New York: Oxford University Press.

Gibson, Katherine, and Kelly Dombroski, eds. 2020. *The Handbook of Diverse Economies*. Cheltenham: Edward Elgar.

Godin, Benoît, and Gérald Gaglio. 2019. 'How Does Innovation Sustain "Sustainable Innovation"?' Pp. 27–37 in *Handbook of sustainable innovation*, edited by F. Boons and A. McMeekin. Cheltenham: Edward Elgar.

Godin, Benoît, Gérald Gaglio, and Dominique Vinck. 2021. 'Introduction to the Handbook on Alternative Theories of Innovation'. Pp. 1–9 in *Handbook on Alternative Theories of Innovation*. Cheltenham: Edward Elgar.

Hayek, Friedrich. 1993. *Law, Legislation, and Liberty, Vol. I: Rules and Order*. London: Routledge.

International Labour Organization. 2018. *Care Work and Care Jobs for the Future of Decent Work*. Geneva: International Labour Office.

Klamer, Arjo, Deirdre N. McCloskey, and Robert M. Solow. 1989. *The Consequences of Economic Rhetoric*. Cambridge: Cambridge University Press.

Lash, Scott, and John Urry. 1994. *Economies of Signs and Space*. London; Thousand Oaks: Sage.

Levy, David L., and André Spicer. 2013. 'Contested Imaginaries and the Cultural Political Economy of Climate Change'. *Organization* 20(5):659–78. https://doi.org/10.1177/1350508413489816.

Maeße, Jens. 2013. 'Das Feld und der Diskurs der Ökonomie'. Pp. 241–75 in *Ökonomie, Diskurs, Regierung*, edited by J. Maeße. Wiesbaden: Springer VS.

Maesse, Jens. 2021. 'Performative, Imaginary and Symbolic Power'. Pp. 19–35 in *Power and Influence of Economists*. London: Routledge.

McCloskey, Deirdre N. 1998. *The Rhetoric of Economics*. 2nd ed. Madison: University of Wisconsin Press.

McGregor, J. Allister, and Nicky Pouw. 2016. 'Towards an Economics of Well-Being'. *Cambridge Journal of Economics*: 1123–42. https://doi.org/10.1093/cje/bew044.

Ötsch, Walter Otto. 2019. *Mythos Markt. Mythos Neoklassik: das Elend des Marktfundamentalismus*. Marburg: Metropolis.

Ötsch, Walter Otto, and Silja Graupe, eds. 2018. *Macht der Bilder, Macht der Sprache*. Neu-Isenburg: Angelika Lenz Verlag.

Ötsch, Walter Otto, and Silja Graupe, eds. 2020. *Imagination Und Bildlichkeit Der Wirtschaft. Zur Geschichte Und Aktualität Imaginierter Fähigkeiten in Der Ökonomie*. Wiesbaden: Springer.

Ray, Larry J., and R. Andrew Sayer, eds. 1999. *Culture and Economy after the Cultural Turn*. London: SAGE.

Schmidt-Wellenburg, Christian, and Frédéric Lebaron. 2018. 'There Is No Such Thing as "the Economy". Economic Phenomena Analysed from a Field-Theoretical Perspective'. *Historical Social Research/Historische Sozialforschung* 43(3):7–38. https://doi.org/10.12759/HSR.43.2018.3.7-38.

Schwarz, H. 2019. 'Arbiträr'. In *Historisches Wörterbuch der Philosophie A-C*, edited by J. Ritter. Damrstadt: Wissenschaftliche Buchgesellschaft.

Searle, John R. 2010. *Making the Social World: The Structure of Human Civilization*. Oxford: Oxford University Press.

Shiller, Robert J. 2019. *Narrative Economics: How Stories Go Viral and Drive Major Economic Events*. Princeton: Princeton University Press.

Sum, Ngai-Ling, and Bob Jessop. 2013. *Towards a Cultural Political Economy: Putting Culture in Its Place in Political Economy*. Cheltenham: Edward Elgar.

Svetlova, Ekaterina. 2008. *Sinnstiftung in der Ökonomik: wirtschaftliches Handeln aus sozialphilosophischer Sicht*. Bielefeld: transcript.

Svetlova, Ekaterina. 2010. 'Unternehmer als Sinnstifter – Macht das Sinn?'. Pp. 165–79 in *Sinnstiftung als Beruf*, edited by M. N. Ebertz and R. Schützeichel. Wiesbaden: Springer VS.

Svetlova, Ekaterina. 2016. 'Performativity and Emergence of Institutions'. Pp. 183–200 in *Enacting Dismal Science: New Perspectives on the Performativity of Economics, Perspectives from Social Economics*, edited by I. Boldyrev and E. Svetlova. New York: Palgrave Macmillan.

Swoyer, Chris. 2015. 'The Linguistic Relativity Hypothesis'. *Stanford Encyclopedia of Philosophy*. Online (last access on march 28th 2023): https://plato.stanford.edu/archives/sum2015/entries/relativism/supplement2.html

Tejani, Sheba. 2019. 'What's Feminist about Feminist Economics?'. *Journal of Economic Methodology* 26(2):99–117. https://doi.org/10.1080/1350178X.2018.1556799.

Waring, Marilyn. 1988. *If Women Counted: A New Feminist Economics*. San Francisco: Harper & Row.

Weick, Karl E. 1995. *Sensemaking in Organizations*. Thousand Oaks: Sage Publications.

6   Grounded economics

If 'the economy' is the ever-changing product of a social process of sense-making in relation to the lifeworld as outlined in Chapters 2 to 5, there arises the question of how to deal with these processes (and respective products) scientifically. As laid out in the introduction and exemplified in this chapter, large parts of standard economics are not interested in such an endeavour in the first place. The chapter will argue that, even if it were interested in entering an open dialogue with social reality, its handed-down methodical toolbox would not allow it to do so. This is why, both in methodical and theoretical terms, a new approach is needed. In other words, we will explore the case for a Grounded Economics.

Standard economics and the lifeworld

The social sciences are devoted to the processes of human coexistence. If these processes always unfold in relation to the lifeworld and the reference is made on the basis of a sphere of meaning, then human sense-making procedures become the central object of social science research and thus also of economic science research. Social reality can then be described as the (always only-situational) product of these processes. Nevertheless, the analytical perspective proposed here is less interested in the intermediate products, but rather, in the active production process of social meaning (cf. Svetlova 2008:172–73; Pratten 2013; Baggio 2020; Graupe 2007; Sum and Jessop 2013). The formula 'no products without a productive process' gives rise to a primacy of becoming instead of being. Guiding questions are: How and on what basis do people cope with life-worldly situations? How are the respective social imaginaries produced, passed on and changed? Anyone interested in the tangible and thus real processes of human coexistence must answer these questions in some way. In fact, they have been answered in the most diverse ways – more or less explicitly – in social philosophy, the social sciences and thus also in economics. Many of these answers have been, or even aimed at, undermining the productive and in principle unfinished activity of human sense-making (cf. Unger 1978, 1987; Graupe 2016). Rigid research designs and methodical assumptions more often than

DOI: 10.4324/9781003371687-6

not drastically limit what can be approached as an object at all, before or during research (Fricker 2007). In this way, however, a loss of the subject matter at hand threatens to lead to meaningless scientific research in the literal sense of the word: one that does not relate to a phenomenon in the lifeworld (cf. Lawson 1987:965).

I want to illustrate this point by presenting the research that economics has brought forward with regard to the formation of its very own identity; that is, the nature and impact of its own educational programmes. The self-reflexive efforts of the discipline show that it cannot even gain a realistic account of a subject matter as familiar to itself as it gets.

With regard to economic higher education, two main strands of research can be identified, both revealing the limitations as outlined before: while one strand pursues the question of whether (future) economists tend to decide differently in comparison to other populations with the help of standardised surveys,[1] another strand relies on experiential research methods as developed by the behavioural sciences.[2] Both approaches deprive themselves of the possibility of capturing lived processes of sense-making that real agents display in real situations at the moment of choosing methods. For example, the powerful reference study by Frey, Pommerehne, and Gygi (1993) explores the question of significantly greater selfishness among economics students in Zurich and West Berlin (compared to the responses of households in both cities):

> At a sight-seeing point, reachable only by foot, a well has been tapped. The bottled water is sold to thirsty hikers. The price is on Swiss franc (SFr) or one German mark (DM) per bottle. Daily production and therewith the stock are 100 bottles. On a particularly hot day, the supplier raises the price to SFr/DM 2 per bottle. How do you evaluate this price rise?
>
> 1. completely fair
> 2. acceptable
> 3. unfair
> 4. very unfair
>
> (Frey, Pommerehne, and Gygi 1993:273–74; see also Haucap and Just 2010)

On the one hand, it remains questionable what the selection from a set of four predefined answer options in relation to a fictitious decision-making situation can say about the moral attitudes that manifest themselves in the everyday considerations or habits of the study's participants. On the other hand, it remains completely unclear which *specific reasons* account for the possibly different answers. For, from the agent's perspective, studying economics is not simply a kind of characteristic that adheres to him or her but a reality that he or she tackles on a daily basis. Instead of taking the direct route and asking respondents about these reasons, standardised procedures rely on specifying *possible* reasons in the form of hypotheses and testing them. Frey, Pommerehne, and Gygi (1993:272) refer back to Marwell and Ames (1981), who introduced the self-selection hypothesis and the indoctrination hypothesis, which have been used repeatedly in further research discourse (see the literature reviews and synthesising studies by Hellmich 2019; Lenger and Buchner 2018; Enste, Haferkamp, and Fetchenhauer 2009). The former explains differences in the population of economics students compared to other populations through latent dispositions that are already present *before* studying and are responsible for an affinity with regard to the choice of economics. The latter explains the differences through formative influences through the 'treatment' of the *study programme itself*. Whether these hypotheses are sufficient to do justice to the variety of possible reasons for divergent moral evaluations in and by different groups may be doubted (independent of the question of *how exactly* this divergence was determined).

A similar criticism can be levelled against behavioural science experiments (with reference to a residual form of individuality and identity in the context of game theoretical experiments see Davis 2011:5; cf. Johnson 2019; Klein et al. 2012). On the one hand, in order to successfully meet their own criteria, these experiments must create a controlled situation that is identical for all participants (cf. the respective instructions as documented in Böhme 2016). The majority[3] of the behaviouralist literature on the 'typical' behaviour of economics students starts with the sterilisation of what is actually of interest here: references to the lifeworld.[4] And even the decision-making situation lacks any foundation in the everyday life of the decision-makers. Thus, the researchers gain a picture of how people behave on the day of the survey in an artificially arranged laboratory situation on a university campus. However, the significance of this gain in knowledge for decisions (and other existential decisions of probands) outside the laboratory situation must be assessed as limited (cf. Frollová, Vranka, and Houdek 2021). Instead of dealing with supposedly objectively valid facts on people's behaviour in the world, they create new social realities through their interventions, in which nothing other than the (in this case, unreflected) primacy of process over being manifests itself. After an in-depth meta-analysis of the research context concerned here, Hellmich (2019:15) summarises:

> Most standard lab settings - such as most of those used here - are not designed to be generalizable to any specific situation in the field or to make substantial predictions of any category of situations. They are intended to reveal basic mechanisms and regularities of economic decisions (Camerer 2015). The experiments used here probably show that being trained in economics can make a difference. But they provide no reliable evidence that people trained in economics generally behave more self-serving, distrusting, and so forth, in the field.

Certainly, one important aspect of the popularity of survey and experimental research might lay with its capacity to provide unambiguous evaluations with the help of statistical procedures. However, the price for this unambiguousness lies in the methodological ignorance of everything that makes decisions significant for real people: their contextuality. Debates such as those about self-selection versus indoctrination hypotheses thus run the risk of becoming phantom debates that bypass the actual orientation problems and sense-making processes of real agents. And indeed, a remarkable number of the standardised studies mentioned above conclude by relativising the results and conceding at least implicitly an ignorance regarding the actual processes of the agents' sense-making procedures: "The gender effect is an interesting phenomenon but it is not clear what are the reasons behind it. The same is true for the education effect and for the fact that it is restricted to male students. Here, too, further research is necessary" (Selten and Ockenfels 1998:532; see also Kroncke 1993:344; Carter and Irons 1991:177; Iida and Oda 2011:238). These examples underline that the choice of method is not a subordinate one, but rather, essentially determines what can still be revealed as an object by the scientist. At least with reference to this research topic (a rather intimate one for fellow economists, one could assume), the aspects of lived reality surviving the epistemic process can be characterised as extremely limited, if not distorted.

After all, it could be said that survey or behavioural research is at least based on the impulses of living people. Although it plays a subordinate role in the research literature on economic higher education, it should be noted against this background that this facet is missing in the so-called 'identity approach' developed by Akerlof and Kranton (2000, 2005, 2010). The approach follows the model-platonic tradition of neoclassical economics (H. Albert 1963) and, without an explicit methodological examination, proceeds by developing a model of the choice of identity; that is, of processes of making sense of oneself. Here, agents are assigned a utility function and a preference order with regard to given identity options, which then enables these modelled agents to make an unambiguous choice at the moment of decision between given identity alternatives:

We propose the following utility function:

(1) $U_j = U_j (\mathbf{a}_j, \mathbf{a}_{-j}, I_j)$.

Utility depends on j's identity or self-image I_j, as well as on the usual vectors of j's actions, $\mathbf{a}_j$, and others' actions, $\mathbf{a}_{-j}$. Since $\mathbf{a}_j$ and $\mathbf{a}_{-j}$ determine j's consumption of goods and services, these arguments and U_j ($\cdot$) are sufficient to capture the standard economics of own actions and externalities.

(Akerlof and Kranton 2000:719)

'Identity' is reduced, in essence, to a (further) utility option and is in turn modelled as follows:

> Following our discussion above, we propose the following representation of I_j:
>
> (2) $I_j = I_j(\mathbf{a}_j, \mathbf{a}_{-j}; \mathbf{c}_j, \boldsymbol{\mathcal{E}}_j, \mathbf{P})$.
>
> A person j's identity I_j depends, first of all, on j's assigned social categories $\mathbf{c}_j$. The social status of a category is given by the function $I_j(\cdot)$, and a person assigned a category with higher social status may enjoy an enhanced self-image. Identity further depends on the extent to which j's own given characteristics e_j match the ideal of j's assigned category, indicated by the prescriptions $\mathbf{P}$. Finally, identity depends on the extent to which j's own and others' actions correspond to prescribed behaviour indicated by $\mathbf{P}$. We call increases or decreases in utility that derive from Ij, *gains or losses in identity*.
>
> (Akerlof and Kranton 2000:719)

Through the complete modelling containment of what 'identity' or 'social status' may still mean for fully 'characterised' agents provided with 'social categories' and the assumption that the decisive individual is thereby subject to a quasi-natural mechanism of fear reduction (cf. Akerlof and Kranton 2000:728), individual behaviour then becomes clearly determinable and predictable: "In the simplest case, an individual j chooses actions to maximize utility (1), taking as given $\mathbf{c}_j$, e_j, and $\mathbf{P}$ and the actions of others" (Akerlof and Kranton 2000:719). By retreating completely into an imagined world, one can reduce the possible processes of identity formation to a single one (constrained optimisation) and also to anticipate the outcome of this choice qua modelled configuration. This approach has been used in particular in the discourse on the economics of education (cf. Akerlof and Kranton 2002). In these scenarios, imagined students quasi-mechanically choose those 'identity options' as provided by educational institutions that promise maximum utility, taking into account their modelled characteristics and their fit with those of the modelled environment. In its original formulation, it lacks any empirical anchoring.[5] If 'reality' in the two abovementioned research strands could only appear in a very abbreviated or deformed form, it is entirely excluded here (cf. Davis 2006:2.1, 2011:4; Fine 2008).[6] To be certain, in all the aforementioned basic texts of identity economics, introductory references are made to real contexts or phenomena of sense-making. However, these enjoy at best a cursory character. The modelling of identity choice always occurs without a (methodologically induced) reference to the lifeworld.

The three methodological traditions within standard economics – as outlined, taking the example of literature on the becoming of economics as discipline itself – all reveal a problematic if not distorted relationship to the lifeworld. Before we address the question of how the discipline could re-relate to the lifeworld, it has to be highlighted that all the confinements of the scientific object that have just been discussed are to be seen as valuations, on which essentially depends what can still appear in the research process as well as in the results. Hence, excluding lived reality from the epistemic process is not only a matter of sound compliance with established traditions but an existential decision made and to-be-legitimised *in front of the rest of the world* by the respective scientist again and again. Bush brings together examples:

> 1) the identification of problems for inquiry as an expression of human interests; 2) the choice of an appropriate logic (or logics) to be used in the formulation of theoretical concepts; 3) the choice and application of a standard (or standards) of relevance in the process of abstraction; 4) the choice of appropriate techniques of empirical observation; 5) the choice and application of a standard (or standards) of statistical significance; 6) the choice of technique (or techniques) by which linguistic and historical dimensions of both the problem and the investigator are to be brought to the fore and subjected to critique; and 7) the choice and application of standards by which to monitor and clarify discourse among the community of scholars involved in the inquiry.
>
> (Bush 1993:91–92)

More often than not, these normative, methodological and methodical decisions are at best implicitly addressed in the research process; for instance, in its linguistic expression in the form of publications, etc. This creates the impression that a problem or phenomenon should be dealt with in *this way* (and not in another). Not infrequently, it is even claimed that a phenomenon *is* the way it is presented in scientific work. Through the identification of the phenomenon and the scientific interpretation of the same, the primordial gap is tried to being closed. The impression is created that the scientific *epistemai* are identical with the lifeworldly *ontos*. Such an account fails to recognise that the scientific interpretations of the lifeworld is also a subordinate one and that an ultimate fit can never be achieved.[7]

Often, in this illusory endeavour, that which should be investigated in the first place is missed, lost or outright destroyed (cf. Brodbeck 2012:80). The tradition dating back to Husserl's *Krisis*, published in 1936, made this alienation from or even loss of the lifeworld the central reproach of the modern, short-sighted ideal of science. Standard economic research can be cited as a prime example of this loss (cf. Düppe 2009). To gain (and retain) a social scientific object means to establish an epistemic relationship towards lifeworldly phenomena.

Re-relating economic science

Social and thus also economic processes gain an eminently *potential* character through the framework as provided in Chapters 2–4. They can be and bring about – to put it in a deliberately unspecific formula – 'many things'. The task of the social scientist – and thus, for the economist – consists in approaching concrete practices and institutions (for example in a company, a nation, an educational context) with a fundamental openness. Knowing that, in the empirical context, many and diverse things can appear, it is up to them to reconstruct and name the actually enacted institutions. How strongly are practices permeated by reflections? How strongly is the agency of the agents involved? Do these practices occur within the confines of institutionalised patterns or do they attempt to transcend them? Such questions help social scientists grasp the development of social and economic realities, at least in terms of a tendency. The model offered in Chapters 2–4 may help as an orientation but should not lead to a model-platonic complacency. It is necessary to develop forms of linguistic, formal and/or graphic representation appropriate to the concrete object at hand. It must be possible to locate specific sense-making processes of a type, group or individual case in them. They can also help identify possible institutional conflicts or frictions of institutional change.

This chapter will offer a methodology oriented around the quest to allow a social phenomenon to show itself and be investigated upon and represented according to its own standards. Instead of limiting or even submerging what can show itself as social reality in advance through the research design to such an extent that the subject matter is lost, economic science can (and should!) establish new epistemic relationships to the socio-ecological arena it is inescapably embedded in (Beker 2022; Schlaudt 2022). In this vein, economics can benefit from Grounded Theorizing as most prominently developed by Barney Glaser and Anselm Strauss (1967), who set out to overcome the gap between 'grand theory', on the one hand, and empirical phenomena, on the other. Instead of applying Glaser and Strauss' approach to economics (Finch 2002; cf. Lee 2005, 2016), the general ethos, the relationship of science and lifeworld as embedded in 'Grounded Theory' shall be emphasised. 'Theory from data' (Glaser and Strauss 1967:1) introduces a primacy of the latter and is generally interested in closing the "gap between highly abstract theory and the multitude of miniscule substantive studies" (Glaser and Strauss 1967:97). As the German translation of Grounded Theory (*gegenstandsbezogene Theorie*) highlights, the approach is built around a subject matter in question, addressing it by means of respective methods, aiming at substantial concepts and theories built from the phenomena approached 'out there'. While it was originally formulated as an inspiration for qualitative social research, it should be pointed out here that this general ethos may well orient quantitative social research respectively (cf. Glaser 2008). 'Grounded Economics' is an attempt to follow this general example in formulating a way of 'doing economics', starting from caring *about*, maybe even caring *for* (cf. Noddings 2002), the lifeworld and its aspects, rather than caring about and for *itself*, its tradition and its institutionalised striving for creating the world in its own image (cf. Chapter 1).

The most important step in this direction is the recognition of the fact that scientific practice is always situated in the lifeworld. It is part of and 'in' the lifeworld, never above or outside it. In the concert of possible references to the lifeworld and its phenomenal manifestations (for example, in the form of interacting people), social scientists are not granted a loge seat. They cannot place themselves outside the lifeworld in order to then 'look back', as it were, on worldly phenomena from this imaginative place (cf. Archer 2000:23). In the end, the meaning of science always unfolds in its relationship to the lifeworld, and the more this relationship is brought into focus, the more 'meaningful' the scientific endeavour becomes – especially for non-scientists. This means that scientists are always positioned in relation to the questions formulated by Bush, above. Scientific practice is always at the same time a normative practice because a certain position is taken. There is no 'view from nowhere' (Nagel 1986):

> there are no absolute starting points, no self-evident, self-contained certainties on which we can build, because we always find ourselves in the middle of complex situations which we try to disentangle by making, then revising, provisional assumptions. This circularity – or perhaps one might call it a spiral approximation towards greater accuracy and knowledge – pervades our whole intellectual life.
> (Rickman 1976:11; cit. as in Mirowski 1987:1010;
> see also Unger 1987)

This does not mean, however, that one stands *anywhere* and cannot devote oneself scientifically to a research object in question. Rather, scientists must deliberate and decide on proper normative (and respective institutional) structures – 'proper' with respect to a scientific norm or goal at hand.[8] In our case, setting out to 'ground' economics, a double opening of economic science shall be formulated as underlaying norms:

- *Transparency*. On the one hand, social scientists can and must communicate what they actually do. They must verbalise their own practice in order to enable others not only to imitate it, but also to critically examine their engagement with the subject matter. An essential component of this explication is what is commonly referred to as research interest, i.e., the motivational background at stake in research. After all, the research interest defines the specific phenomenon to which an epistemic relationship is (to be) established. The choice of method is then an expression of precisely this research interest, and its implementation is to be documented. To be capable of such disclosure means to be able to justify (and defend) one's research in principle. To do so is to enable and promote a transparent engagement with one's work.
- *Epistemic justice*. On the other hand, social scientists can and must enable their subject matter, that is the people who (re)produce meaning in their contexts, to show themselves as they want in relation to the researchers'

epistemic interest. There is no doubt that the epistemic relationship between social scientists and the phenomena they are interested in is usually raised by the former and that the process is accordingly structured to a large extent by them. However, no right can be derived from this initiative to overhaul the phenomenon of interest with one's own interpretations.[9] Statements about a social, human phenomenon must be grounded in the statements and positions of the *people themselves* and not in those of the scientists. Second-degree interpretations, i.e., scientific interpretations, always refer to first-degree interpretations, i.e., those of the agents, which must be taken seriously as such and not derived from the former. It is an interested (Lat. *inter-esse* = to be in between) and a serving function that social scientists take, not an overriding one.

Scientific freedom, as both norms formulated here suggest, finds a limit in the lived freedom of the people being studied – i.e., the sense-making agents. Among other things, this can also mean that the success of research is not evaluated and assessed solely by scientists but also and increasingly by the agents themselves. Scientific freedom, which can also be read and practised as arbitrariness, is supplemented here by the ethos of *epistemic justice* (cf. Fricker 2007).[10] As social scientists, we are responsible for doing justice to the phenomena to which we devote ourselves. Our research does not move in a vacuum - it always already relates to the existential excitations of living people. This existentiality of the scientific counterpart demands an ethical decision, or attitude. As already indicated above, such a normative dimension lies, at the same time, in the unlimited richness of alternatives of our references to the counterpart. I can devote myself to economic reality in *one way or another*. I am responsible for this decision. This means, for example, with regard to the question of the adequacy of various conceptions of individuality, that these must be developed and answered for not in the light of methodological deliberations but in relation to living people (cf. Davis 2011:17).

After all, the existentiality of the scientific counterpart is also reflected in the conditions of possibility of (economic) scientific research itself. In order to be carried out, it is dependent on the legacies of human sense-making and institution-building, be it in the form of language or the possibilities of academic institutions. Without referring to these existential backgrounds of social research in one way or another, it will sooner or later become meaningless, due to its oblivion of the sources of its very own meaning and existence (cf. Düppe 2009:24; Wisman 1979:24). Conversely, the limitation of scientific freedom through a responsible relationship towards phenomena holds out the prospect of a fullness of meaning in scientific practice and knowledge. Doing research in a conscious relationship to real-world phenomena is always an activity at the ravages of time. If this endeavour succeeds, the challenge of 'knowledge transfer' becomes easier and the meaning and purpose of social science research more comprehensible to a non-academic audience. If I am investigating, for instance, the supposed self-transformation procedures of economics students, doing research equals doing justice to the sense-making practices of real people I am interested in. This is tantamount to taking them seriously with regard to what, how and why they do things as they do.

With the introduction of epistemic justice, the presumptuousness of the endeavour to elevate one certain interpretation to the rank of a space- and timeless truth becomes ever clearer. Not only does such an attempt conceal the always-prevailing plenitude of human interpretative achievements and possibilities; rather, it closes the principally unfinished and open reference to the lifeworld and buries the phenomenal plenitude under the proclaimed truth (cf. Unger and Smolin 2015:70–72). These and other forms of epistemic injustice are possible, but ultimately illusionary, since even the negation of the lifeworld still represents a lifeworldly relationship and is thus always raised or motivated by a lifeworldly situatedness. Modern science, including economics, made this negation its very condition of existence: "the problem of modern science is that its *practice is the oblivion of the motives that give rise to it*" (Düppe 2009:2; see also Unger 1978, 1987).

A prominent indicator of the ever-embeddedness of the social scientific endeavour is the interpretative means it is dependent on. Social scientists are not only always 'in the same space and time' through their sheer co-existence with their research objects. The means of their scientific debate are also ultimately mediated by everyday, pre-scientific references to the lifeworld. In their explanatory, understanding, observing and analysing approaches to the lifeworld, social scientists always rely on *other*, non-scientific social imaginaries: "even economists are human beings, and cannot divest themselves of human habits of thought" (Robinson 2021:54; see also McCloskey 2000:1–2). Their methods and explanations build on general patterns of communication, interpretation and observation that science itself does not produce, but unquestionably uses. The giant Newton stood on is to be conceived of not just as an aggregate of genius thinkers but as a general cultural current (including language, frames, institutions, artefacts, norms, etc.) having allowed him to see what he saw. In other words, science and scientists have a past that they cannot *performatively* get rid of but on which they depend in order to scientifically relate to the lifeworld:

> Husserl's thesis of science presupposing the life-world means that science is phenomenologically *late*. Before there is an interest to adopt a scientific attitude, before a scientific practice can be instituted and carried out, already a lot of sense-labor (*Sinnarbeit*) had to take place. Science is not 'self-made'. Before we are able to claim scientific authority, we already acquired a great deal of the world by means of such acts as reminding, associating, apprehending, anticipating, expecting, being attracted, driven, repulsed or appealed, and other 'primordial' forms of motivations that make experiences 'lived' (Hua. XI). An epistemic interest is something that has

to become. It has to grow. The practice of science is phenomenologically old. Science has a *past.*

(Düppe 2009:18)

If human references are already existentially late, since they always refer to an already preceding lifeworld, then (social) scientific interpretations are *doubly* late, insofar as they represent new references (in the form of scientific knowledge), which in turn are already based on other references. There is no 'everyday knowledge' without the lifeworld and no scientific knowledge without everyday knowledge. Social scientific knowledge is about interpretations of interpretations; it is 'second-degree constructions' (Schütz 1971:7):

> Interpretation must mediate between one context and another. We have no external place, untainted by presuppositions, from which we can undertake social study. As we never escape pre-interpretation, it is healthy to respect this and not minimise interpretative difficulties or brush them aside. Problems of pre-interpretation mean that social studies are daunting and recondite, but not impossible, and need interpretative skills from the researcher.
>
> (Jackson 2009:146; see also Lavoie 1991; Gerrard 1993)

This is especially true for the fundamental motives that trigger academic work in the first place. Beginning with the marginalist revolution and carried forward by what Paul Samuelson was to call 'Modern Mainstream Economics' (cf. Cherrier 2016), a considerable proportion of academically based economists have done their utmost to deny its origins: "the indifference to the very concern of meaning seems to guarantee the economists' discursive identity" (Düppe 2009:39). The repositioning of economic science in and out of tangible practice is therefore only possible at the price of its fundamental – i.e., paradigmatic – repositioning.

Method in grounded economics

Research in Grounded Economics takes on a serving function in the notion proposed here; its task is to do epistemic justice to an economic phenomenon in question (Beker 2022; Hodgson 2004:447–48). In this respect, an old credo of Alfred Marshall's should be emphasised,[11] not only for the agents themselves, but also for researchers. They, too, may discover their guiding star in the everyday experiences of living people. In order to meet this demand, they must make their choice of methods in close assessment and knowledge of this living subject matter. This process always involves turning towards the subject matter, and only from there can a successive distancing and methodologically controlled abstraction be initiated. As Grounded Economics, it sets out to reconstruct the multifaceted practices that condition the (re)production of the institutions prevailing in the respective context.

Grounded Economics is always *empirical* research in the word's original sense. It follows living peoples' experiences and tries to understand them (Lat. *empiricus*: following experience; cf. on an empirical foundation of economic science Shackle (1992:VI)). The mode of these individual as well as the collective experiences is practice: a performative way of dealing with lifeworldly situations. In these practices, they (re)produce institutions that allow for a stable way of dealing with the lifeworld. Against this background, in addition to the products of this process, the performative (re)production process of the same always forms part of the phenomenal area of interest. Grounded Economics is always also interested in the generative patterns of economic realities. It develops a "genetic account of an unfolding process" (Veblen 1898:388).

The identification as an empirical research approach is not to be understood as a principled rejection of modelling procedures, but rather, as a decisive rejection of any form of model Platonism (cf. Albert 1963), regardless of whether they are formal, linguistic, pictorial or otherwise. Scientific interpretations are second-degree interpretations. In order to attain meaning, they *must* refer to first-degree interpretations (i.e., the performative sense-making processes of agents 'out there') and in such a way that one can actually do justice to the latter. Both processes of interpretation are always situated in the lifeworld and are not abstract simulations in the scientist's head. Thus, scientificity is not guaranteed by the choice of normalised or dubbed 'scientific' research methods, as standard economic textbooks still tend to present it (cf. Mankiw 2021:18). In the context of Grounded Economics, scientificity is indicated by a resonant relationship between scientific and lived meaning 'out there'. This relationship quality will be introduced as the operationalisable criterion of adequacy (see the following).

What a Grounded Economist then encounters in the course of her work is not a principled, but a lived abundance of human meaning as present in economic action:

> Economic activity is a logically (rationally) untraceable practice that can be theoretically mapped with the help of the concepts of sense-making. . . . The conversion of theory to the sense-making that takes place in performative practices requires the abandonment of the logocentric two-world model in which thought is the cause of action. Doing business happens in the act of doing, *while* acting, deciding and talking; in the act of doing, which makes intentions ineffective and decisions possible in the first place.
> (Svetlova 2008:191)

In this sense, the lifeworld is not subordinated in the sense of an *economics of life* to a single horizon of meaning; for example, in the form of a rationalist decision-making programme (cf. Becker and Nashat 1997). In contrast to the established conventions of economics, turning to the lived diversity of economic social imaginaries requires a fundamental epistemic openness (cf. Mulgan 2021). With its means and approaches, such research does not set a meaning for economic action but methodically maintains an openness to what the economy may mean for the agents (re)producing it. Only in this way can it hold out the prospect of understanding of how 'the economy' is actually produced by living agents in specific contexts. For instance, one might certainly observe economic practices 'out there', based on highly logical or rational thinking (or planning). Yet, standard economic theory would fall short of approaching them in a grounded way, since it conceptualises rational action (or decision-making) not as merely a *possible* but as *the only* form of action. Additionally, it is not able to reconstruct rational action in its quality as a meaningful reference to the lifeworld.

Methodically, the openness called for means that Grounded Economists must be able to choose from a wide plurality of potential approaches to social practices and the institutions that manifest themselves in them. This plurality undoubtedly includes qualitative – such as reconstructive or ethnographic – methods (cf. Flick 2014; Lune and Berg 2017) which open up a *relatively* unmediated access to lived institutionalisations (cf. Schlüter 2010). Although the discipline's core largely ignores or even rejects these possibilities (cf. Lenger 2019), a large number of potential role models for such work can be identified in relation to spatio-temporally broad or narrowly ramified economic phenomena (cf. Starr 2014:4; Basole and Ramnarain 2016; as well as in part Lee and Cronin 2016:III). Examples can be found in such diverse approaches and areas of research as multi-level analyses of municipal debt (cf. Deruytter and Möller 2020), research on digitally mediated consumer behaviour (cf. Lamla 2009) or the investigation of corporate risk assessment of supply chains by means of case studies (cf. Blome and Schoenherr 2011; see also Srinivas 2020; Ostrom 2005; Tuckett 2012; Gibson and Dombroski 2020).

It is, of course, also possible to quantify economic practices. It is *one* possible form of second-degree interpretations among many to count them or put them into quantitative relationships, which makes them accessible to methods of quantitative (empirical) social research. Especially in the case of quantified or quantifying practices 'out there', a corresponding choice of method is obvious, since there is a familiarity between first- and second-degree interpretations. Quantitative methods also have the advantage of allowing for the assessment of relatively large samples. In this respect, the decisive factor in the decision for quantitative methods (as well as for all other methods) is not a disciplinary fashion or tradition but the suitability for understanding real-world economic practices. Yet, the possibility and availability of quantitative methods should not obscure the fact that economic practices can never be understood exhaustively, often not even adequately, with the help of quantitative methods. As the *Social Studies of Quantification* (cf. Mennicken and Espeland 2019) equally emphasise and prove, this is especially true for quantifying practices 'out there'. This warning is essentially related to the methodologically induced abstraction from non-countable aspects of social processes. For the decision in favour of counting and calculating brings with it limitations that mean that decisive aspects of social reality cannot come into the view of scientific consideration. The examples given at the beginning of this chapter can be regarded as notoriously symptomatic of quantitative research approaches that systematically ignore their methodical limitations and thus ultimately advance to second-degree interpretations that have little in common with those 'out there'. In these cases, more or less reflected epistemic decisions lead to doing justice to disciplinary conventions but not to the phenomenon in question. Positive examples of reflexive and consistently object-oriented quantitative research can be found in fields as diverse as stochastic financial market research (cf. Buchanan, Chai, and Deakin 2020) or inequality research (cf. Dorn, Maxand, and Kneib 2021), quantitative research on networks in companies and organisations (cf. Bakker, Hendriks, and Korzilius 2022) or quantitative narrative research (cf. Snowden 2005; Van der Merwe et al. 2019); for example, in the field of transformative supply chain research (cf. Deprez, Huyghe, and Van Gool Maldonado 2012).

But even where quantitative methods can be used to address central aspects of a phenomenon, they are usually not sufficient to understand it adequately from a praxeological point of view. For example, quantitative-empirical inequality research provides precise information on the fact that women earn less than men in a certain period of time in a certain place or in a certain sector. However, a sufficient understanding of the phenomenon 'gender pay gap' requires not only its identification (what?) and extension (how much?) but also, for instance, an examination of the institutional conditions and processes of its existence (why? how?), or its significance in and for the life reality of the stakeholders involved (who?). These generative processes can only be understood with a comprehensive view of the economic practices *behind the numbers*. The decision *against* (as well as for) such a comprehensive view is a normative one – the supposed value-free nature of quantitative methods should not obscure this: "As political economists we are political agents when we define, and reproduce, our object of study. We face both an analytical and a normative imperative to work with and towards statistics that do justice to the world and the people in it" (Mügge 2020:1).

This systematic point can be illustrated directly by the example of the research practice of quantitative methods itself: in order for it to become meaningfully *itself*, quantitative research *must be* placed in non-numerical contexts of meaning. The textuality or pictoriality (for example in the form of graphs) of respective publications are one example; the discursive explanation of research at scientific conferences or in public interventions is another (Greiffenhagen, Mair, and Sharrock 2011). These contextualisations of numbers are no triviality. Without this referencing, quantitative research *must* necessarily remain meaningless (cf. Lawson 1987:965) and it cannot be realised without recourse to non-quantitative medialities (cf. Pickbourn and Ramnarain 2016).

Understanding the meaning of an institution or a process of institutionalisation thus requires a plurality of epistemic approaches and medialities. An effective expression of this insight may be seen in integrated procedures, as they are negotiated under the term of mixed-methods research (see Cronin 2016; as well as the examples of Keske et al. 2011; Stumpf, Schöggl, and Baumgartner 2021).

In the context of Grounded Economics, however, such a pluralism of methods does not become an abstract end in itself but a necessity in order to do justice to an ambiguous social reality. A pluralism of methods receives its meaningfulness in the relationship between science and a phenomenon, both bound together and ultimately referring to the lifeworld. Against this backdrop, methodical innovations will be a rule rather than an exception of a Grounded research process (Kara 2020). This is not an argument against methodical rigor but certainly against methodical canonisations. Centring the research process around phenomena will render such ambitions dysfunctional and an expression of epistemic injustice.

But who can actually judge whether what is essential and in question has actually been recognised? This question touches on the criteria of social scientific practice, which are to be obtained here in a deliberately general version for the programme of a Grounded Economics, following Schütz and the tradition of reconstructive social research. As a central criterion of social science research and in accordance with what has already been elaborated, Schütz proposes that of 'adequacy' and states:

> Each term in a scientific model of human action must be constructed in such a way that a human act performed within the life-world by an individual actor in the way indicated by the typical construct would be understandable for the actor himself as well as for his fellowmen in terms of common-sense interpretation of everyday life. Compliance with this postulate warrants the consistency of the constructs of the social scientists with the constructs of common-sense experience of the social reality.
>
> (Schütz 1962:44)

Whether an empirical reconstruction of the social imaginaries of actual agents is adequate or valid cannot be judged by a supposedly objective external criterion that could be applied as a golden standard to all reconstruction processes (cf. Przyborski and Wohlrab-Sahr 2021:26–29). This does not mean, however, that this kind of research would turn into arbitrariness. On the contrary, reconstructions must always be able to withstand the decisive test of actually doing justice to the lived processes of sense-making 'out there'. The central criterion of adequacy is thus an eminently relational one. Against the background of an explicated (transparent) interest in knowledge, it aims at a far-reaching overlapping of first- and second-degree interpretations. The expertise of such an assessment is, on the one hand, incumbent on scholars and insiders who are familiar with the field in question as well as with the methodical-methodological examination of it. Ultimately – as Schütz reminds us – the validity of the research results can and must always also be assessed by agents themselves. A research process that is based on human interaction with the lifeworld can and must ultimately be judged in precisely these contexts or be able to prove itself there. For this, it is crucial that the results are prepared so that they can actually be understood in the contexts they are bound to. The decision to communicate agent-sensitively is not an expression of under-complexity but is at least intended to raise the possibility that the agents concerned can form their own judgements about the research findings. This elevates participation (Hecker et al. 2018), science communication (Gregory and Miller 2000) and transdisciplinarity in general (Maasen and Lieven 2006) from a nice-to-have status to an integral part of (social) scientific research. As Chapter 7 will hint at, this close science-society-nexus also proves to be crucial for transformative endeavours.

In addition to the adequacy or validity of second-degree interpretations, their *reliability* in the sense of a methodically controlled reproducibility of the results in repeated surveys should be mentioned as a second important criterion. A *generalisability* of the results obtained to a population exceeding the empirical basis is possible, in principle, if appropriate procedures – especially of sampling – are respected (cf. Przyborski and Wohlrab-Sahr 2021, Chapters 2.4, 6). In principle, however, Grounded research, in sharp distinction to the quantitative criterion of representativeness, admonishes that generalising statements should be treated with caution and must not lead to the lived interpretation procedures being overridden by ontologisations of any kind.

Theory in Grounded Economics

Grounded Economics does not lose itself in mere 'data collection'. Its aim is to present empirically sound theories of economic institutions and their constant transformation without hypostasising these theories into space- and timeless truths. Theories have a serving function by offering meaningful text, pictures, etc., for the aspect of social reality in question:

> Theories, phenomenologically speaking, are re-presentations of the world not in that they depict it, but by means of being *presentiations*, that is, expressions of the lived world that gives rise to an epistemic problem in the first place. Theories 'tell' from the world in which they are made.
>
> (Düppe 2009:31)

In this sense, Grounded theories follow the Greek root of *theoria* as *con-ception* (German: *Anschauung*). A Grounded (Glaser and Strauss 1967) or conceptive theory (cf. Schefold 2004), despite its distanced view, is bound to a concrete experience, to specific cases (cf. Hodgson 2003:173). Theory, in the sense of an abstract, decidedly unworldly speculation or intellectual contemplation, is precisely what Grounded Economics tries to avoid (cf. Jackson 2009:162). Because of its empirical grounding, theory-building, in this sense, cannot avoid being pluralistic, at least when the phenomena under investigation are themselves diverse. For this reason, Grounded Economics is never merely reproductive but always also creative research. It creates language and images for something that has not been explicitly been grasped so far. To put it in a methodological term: in its theorising ambition, it follows down an *abductive* pathway and creates second-order interpretations for the processes of sensemaking inherent in a certain phenomenal setting. These interpretations are the expression of a genuine epistemic interest and thus of a scientific attitude: abduction is "not a method, on the basis of which precisely specifiable steps everyone arrives at a certain result, but an *attitude* of actually wanting to *learn* something and not applying what has been learned" (Reichertz 1993:273 ff.; my translation).

In institutionalism, as in the broader field of socioeconomics, reconstructive methods, in general, and abductive theorisation, in particular, are a widely tested procedure (Blosser 2020; Kurrild-Klitgaard 2001; Finch 1997) with correspondingly diverse examples of application and variants (cf. Storper and Salais 1997; Hall and Soskice 2001; Rosser and Rosser 2004; Ostrom 2005; Bollier and Helfrich 2019; Fainshmidt et al. 2018; Bruno and Estrin 2021). However, the consistent realisation of theorisation in and out of lived practices remains a methodological challenge that has not yet been met:

> The conceptual apparatus referred to generally as agency-structure or agency-institution is central to a great deal of social science, not least Institutional Economics. Despite its centrality, this apparatus has never been able to fully explain how institutions and social structures influence agents, encouraging advocates (including myself) to take refuge in deliberately vague phrases like 'institutions and structures condition, govern, influence, or shape agency'.
>
> (Fleetwood 2008:183)

If the economic sciences succeed in mastering this challenge, an understanding of the shape and genesis of institutions might come into sight that does not fall from the sky but has been reconstructed from the lived practices of concrete actors. Such knowledge could also be fed back into the field with transformative intentions for political design processes (cf. Chapter 7). The good news is that economists do not have to reinvent the methodological wheel for such a goal but can learn from developments in neighbouring disciplines that were able to resist (at least in part) the temptations of losing the lifeworld in the course of the 20th century. This refers to the broad field of empirical social research, as (further) developed particularly in sociology, anthropology, educational sciences and psychology and alluded to in the previous section. Such a rapprochement with other social sciences would thus reunite what already has a common origin (cf. Vallet and Pressman 2020) and what has gained increased popularity under the slogan of interdisciplinarity, also in the economic sciences (Klebaner and Montalban 2020; Swedberg et al. 2020; Cruz-e-Silva and Cavalieri 2021).

Just as the pluralism of methods under the guiding star of epistemic justice experiences a restriction with reference to the object in question, a phenomenon-oriented approach also requires a restriction with regard to the pluralism of theories. To be more precise, a principled scepticism is expressed here towards the use of formal techniques and procedures in the theory-building step. This scepticism is based on two arguments:

- A formal type of theory building has to struggle *in principle* with the problem that it is *in actu* dependent on having to abstract from tangible contexts in order to produce a meaningful outcome. Of course, a formal theory of the social can be empirically substantiated or 'tested'. However, such a model ultimately owes its validity not to any relationship to a lifeworldly phenomenon, but to the rules and laws of a formal system of relevance (cf. Unger 2007:97 ff.). The possibilities of formal theories are bought at the price of time, or - in the terminology of the present work - of the lifeworld (cf. Hua VI, § 9). The 'sense' of a formal model is generated at the very same moment it loses the lifeworld. Of course, *ex ante* ('empirical underpinning') or *ex post* ('testing' or 'verbal plausibilisation') references to lifeworldly phenomena can be re-established. However, the formal model *as a formal model* does not gain legitimacy from these relations but from its self-referential, formal relations. Thus, in my opinion, it is not possible to formulate a formal theory of social processes doing justice to a subject matter as outlined in Chapters 2–4 because these processes always occur in an interrelatedness within the lifeworld, from which formal methods must abstract in order to make sense.

- The second argument against formal procedures of theory building focuses on their suggestive effects. Formal expressions foster the impression that the validity of the modelled context goes beyond its intended scope, optionally also beyond the underlying empirical context. As we have just seen, this effect has a systematic origin. And it may very likely result in the omission or even the oblivion of the fundamental openness of social processes.[12] Such openness lies in the uncontrollable agency, or indeterminacy, of the agents who produce 'the economy' in social practices. And it is precisely this agency that is counteracted by the formal suggestion that agents have always had to act as assumed by the model - even when the model was developed strictly empirically.[13] Formal theories suggest a degree of supposed immutability of social processes that is, in my opinion, incompatible with strong conceptions of *agency*. They encourage an oblivion of the essentially non-formal openness of human, and thus social, and thus economic, practices, which restricts or even destroys the scope for action through the multiple effects of science on society (cf. Chapter 1). For their part, language- or image-based techniques also struggle with this problem. In order to generate second-degree interpretations, they depend on making a selection of words or images that can do justice to this context. In the worst case, this selection and its presentation can be made in such a way as to suggest – similar to formal methods – a timeless causality or even a quasi-natural 'law'. However, the dangers are far less because the possibility of voicing contradictions is immediate and given to a much larger number of people than with formally conducted arguments. With the help of the latter, no strong agency can be justified because they *must* miss the essential, non-formalisable characteristic of such agency *in actu*. The second argument, however, does not address the principled impossibility of a formal economic theory doing justice to its subject matter, but rather, its legitimacy on the horizon of its potential effects on social reality. The problem here is not a systematic one but a (research) ethical one.

Against the background of these two arguments, I am sceptical about purely formal as well as hybrid forms of theory building – contrary to the possibilities in early and more immediate stages of interpretation. It is one thing to make social phenomena countable, to count them and analyse them with the help of quantitative methods (cf. Glaser 2008); it is another to hypostatise formal relationships into a theory of the social (or economic). This distinction marks the one already discussed between *epistemai* and *ontos*. While mathematics *as a method* emphasises this distinction because it is *one* way of interpreting the lifeworld, it blurs it when it is *confused* with the lifeworld *as an abstract theory*.

Contrasting the hopes and attitudes as connected with 'high theory', Grounded Theories in economics try to keep alive the link to the phenomena they try to tell of in the sense of Düppe. This implies the imperative to reformulate theories (of banks, of enterprises, of individual decision-making) when the respective phenomenon changes.

Notes

1 See, for instance, Rubinstein (2006), Allgood et al. (2012) or Paxton (2019). See Bäuerle (2022:18) for further literature.
2 See, for instance, Selten and Ockenfels (1998), Wang, Malhotra, and Murnighan (2011) or Kaiser, Pedersen, and Koch (2018). See Bäuerle (2022:19) for further literature.
3 Research designs based on real-life students' decision-making have been developed by Frey and Meier (2003, 2005), Yezer, Goldfarb, and Poppen (1996), O'Roark (2012) and Nowell and Laufer (1997). But here, too, instead of being asked directly, statistical significances with regard to students' observed willingness to donate, their willingness to return a supposedly lost letter or subsequent voting behaviour as MPs in a certain population of students shall reveal supposed underlying mechanisms.
4 See, for example, that and how such references, especially social relationships, are proactively prevented by the survey designs: "It is very important that you do not talk

to any other participant. If you do not follow this rule we will have to exclude you from the experiment and you will not earn any money" (Carter and Irons 1991:172; López-Pérez and Spiegelman 2019:159; see also Selten and Ockenfels 1998:532; Wang, Malhotra, and Murnighan 2011:648).

5 Further developments, for example in the economics of education, usually 'empiricise' the approach with the help of the two aforementioned research approaches: surveys (Clots-Figueras and Masella 2013) or behavioural/neuroscientific experiments (Huettel and Kranton 2012). Cf. with reference to the latter: "Physical laws and neurophysiological states physically allow or limit the manner in which we act. But they do not determine the content of the action, nor the *reasons* which moved us to act in one way instead of another" (Baggio 2020:1671; see also Davis 2010).

6 Davis (2011:197) extends this criticism to the endogenising identity model of Horst, Kirman, and Teschl (2007):

> In effect, their approach, valuable as it is in its recognition of the need to endogenize identity, is too constrained by the mathematics of equilibrium theorizing to generate sufficient behavioural structure to produce any other account of personal identity but the one they anticipate.

7 The maintenance of a categorical difference between interpretations and the world may be regarded as the basic concern of critical realism, as it has been developed in economics, alongside Archer (2000:30), in particular by Tony Lawson (1987, 1997).

8 See, for instance, the classic example of CUDOS norms ('Communism', Universality, Disinterestedness, Organized Skepticism) as formulated by Robert Merton (1973).

9 Transformative research approaches, which aim to change their research objects, are a special case here. To this end, however, they must adhere to a series of research ethical standards, which include an explicit and transparent negotiation of the direction of change, as well as of the process of change, with the involvement and consent of holders of what is at stake (cf. Mertens 2009).

10 More specifically, I refer to Fricker's notion of a 'hermeneutical injustice': "hermeneutical injustice occurs . . . when a gap in collective interpretive resources puts someone at an unfair disadvantage when it comes to making sense of their social experiences" (Fricker 2007, p. 1; cf. in detail ibid., ch. 7). The focus is on the relationship between interpreters and their experiences. Hermeneutic justice exists when the former is able to interpret the latter adequately with the help of their collectively handed down social imaginaries – also in relation to other social groups with other interpretative resources. When applied as a category of (social) science theory, this criterion gains additional significance because the interpreting researchers usually interpret experiences *of others*. Here, the ethical significance of the social, lifeworldly mediated relationship between researcher and research object becomes evident, the naming and negotiation of which is made possible by Fricker's concept. The success of the social scientific endeavour must be proven in the negotiation of the research results with the social agents – not only because they, as the originators of the first-degree interpretations, should be able to judge the legitimacy of the second-degree interpretations but also because, otherwise, an (unjust) knowledge gap would arise between scientists and agents. Successful social sciences always create an epistemic gap in relation to their objects of study, in order to level it out again as far as possible. Transfer, communication and participation are not *add-ons* to the scientific process but become (research) ethical imperatives against the background of epistemic justice. Similar to Fricker, it is a matter of empowering those who usually have little to say in the negotiation of an issue – although the issue immediately concerns them or they may even *be* the issue (cf. economics students). The concept of epistemic justice is closely related to what Matthews (2006) calls 'epistemic humility'.

11 "The common sense of a person who has had a large experience of life will give him more guidance in such a matter than he can gain from subtle economic analysis" (Marshall 1920:56).

12 These suggestive effects of formal methods are not a triviality, but, if one follows Husserl, have a constitutive significance in the historical process of the formation of modern scientificity:

> Mathematics and mathematical science, as a garb of ideas, or the garb of symbols of the symbolic mathematical theories, encompasses everything which, for scientists and the educated generally, *represents* the life-world, *dresses it up* as 'objectively actual and true' nature. It is through the garb of ideas that we take for *true being* what is actually a *method* – a method which is designed for the purpose of progressively improving, *in infinitum*, through 'scientific' predictions, those rough predictions which are the only ones originally possible within the sphere of what is actually experienced and experienceable in the lifeworld. It is because of the disguise of ideas that the true meaning of the method, the formulae, the 'theories,' remained unintelligible and, in the naive formation of the method, was *never* understood.
>
> (Husserl 1984:51–52)

Economics can be seen as a prime example of a science that owes its effectiveness to the nimbus of this suggestion, but at the same time, also a latent meaninglessness or disorientation with regard to its own relation to and in the lifeworld.

13 In fact, habitual practices still offer the greatest possibilities for formalising interpretation ("Whatever we can repeat we express in a formula and then embody in a machine" Unger (2007:42)). Formalising them, however, undermines the possibility of interpreting what happens as a manifestation of other forms of practice. It also undercuts the potentialities of habitual practice itself. Even if they *seem* quasi-automatic, as human practices, they lack formal necessity.

References

Akerlof, George A., and Rachel E. Kranton. 2000. 'Economics and Identity'. *Quarterly Journal of Economics* 115:715–53. https://doi.org/10.1162/003355300554881.

Akerlof, George A., and Rachel E. Kranton. 2002. 'Identity and Schooling: Some Lessons for the Economics of Education'. *Journal of Economic Literature* 40(4):1167–201. https://doi.org/10.1257/002205102762203585.

Akerlof, George A., and Rachel E. Kranton. 2005. 'Identity and the Economics of Organizations'. *Journal of Economic Perspectives* 19(1):9–32. https://doi.org/10.1257/0895330053147930.

Akerlof, George A., and Rachel E. Kranton. 2010. *Identity Economics: How Our Identities Shape Our Work, Wages, and Well-Being.* Princeton: Princeton University Press.

Albert, Hans. 1963. 'Modell-Platonismus. Der Neoklassische Stil Des Ökonomischen Denkens in Kritischer Betrachtung'. Pp. 45–76 in *Sozialwissenschaft und Gesellschaftsgestaltung. Festschrift für Gerhard Weisser*, edited by F. Karrenberg and Hand Albert. Berlin: Duncker & Humblot.

Allgood, Sam, William Bosshardt, Wilbert van der Klaauw, and Michael Watts. 2012. 'Is Economics Coursework, or Majoring in Economics, Associated with Different Civic Behaviors?'. *The Journal of Economic Education* 43:248–68. https://doi.org/10.1080/0 0220485.2012.686389.

Archer, Margaret S. 2000. *Being Human: The Problem of Agency.* Cambridge: Cambridge University Press.

Baggio, Guido. 2020. 'Emergence, Time and Sociality: Comparing Conceptions of Process Ontology'. *Cambridge Journal of Economics* 44(6):1365–94. https://doi.org/10.1093/cje/beaa019.

Bakker, Sabine R., Paul H. Hendriks, and Hubert P. Korzilius. 2022. 'Let It Go or Let It Grow? – Personal Network Development and the Mobilization of Intra-Organizational Social Capital'. *Social Networks* 68:179–94. https://doi.org/10.1016/j.socnet.2021.06.002.

Basole, Amit, and Smita Ramnarain. 2016. 'Qualitative and Ethnographic Methods in Economics'. Pp. 135–64 in *Handbook of Research Methods and Applications in Heterodox Economics*, edited by F. Lee and B. Cronin. Cheltenham: Edward Elgar.

Bäuerle, Lukas. 2022. *Ökonomie – Praxis – Subjektivierung. Eine Praxeologische Institutionenforschung Am Beispiel Ökonomischer Hochschulbildung.* Bielefeld: transcript.

Becker, Gary S., and Guity Nashat. 1997. *The Economics of Life: From Baseball to Affirmative Action to Immigration.* New York: McGraw-Hill.

Beker, Victor A. 2022. *Economics, Social Science and Pluralism: A Real-World Approach.* London: Routledge.

Blome, Constantin, and Tobias Schoenherr. 2011. 'Supply Chain Risk Management in Financial Crises – A Multiple Case-Study Approach'. *International Journal of Production Economics* 134(1):43–57. https://doi.org/10.1016/j.ijpe.2011.01.002.

Blosser, Joe. 2020. 'Relational History: Adam Smith's Types of Human History'. *Erasmus Journal for Philosophy and Economics* 12(2). https://doi.org/10.23941/ejpe.v12i2.419.

Böhme, Juliane. 2016. 'Doing Laboratory Experiments: An Ethnomethodological Study of the Performative Practice in Behavioral Economic Research'. Pp. 87–108 in *Enacting Dismal Science*, edited by I. Boldyrev and E. Svetlova. New York: Palgrave Macmillan.

Bollier, David, and Silke Helfrich. 2019. *Free, Fair and Alive: The Insurgent Power of the Commons.* Gabriola Island: New Society Publishers.

Brodbeck, Karl-Heinz. 2012. *Die Herrschaft Des Geldes. Geschichte Und Systematik.* 2nd ed. Darmstadt: Wissenschaftliche Buchgesellschaft.

Bruno, Randolph Luca, and Saul Estrin. 2021. 'Taxonomies and Typologies: Starting to Reframe Economic Systems'. Pp. 871–96 in *Palgrave Handbook of Comparative Economics*, edited by E. Douarin and O. Havrylyshyn. London: Palgrave Macmillan.

Buchanan, John, Dominic H. Chai, and Simon Deakin. 2020. 'Unexpected Corporate Outcomes from Hedge Fund Activism in Japan'. *Socio-Economic Review* 18(1):31–52. https://doi.org/10.1093/ser/mwy007.

Bush, Paul D. 1993. 'The Methodology of Institutional Economics: A Pragmatic Instrumentalist Perspective'. Pp. 59–107 in *Institutional Economics: Theory, Method, Policy*, edited by M. R. Tool. Boston: Kluwer Academic Publishers.

Carter, John R., and Michael D. Irons. 1991. 'Are Economists Different, and If So, Why?'. *Journal of Economic Perspectives* 5(2):171–77. https://doi.org/10.1257/jep.5.2.171.

Cherrier, Beatrice. 2016. 'How the Term "Mainstream Economics" Became Mainstream: A Speculation'. *Institute for New Economic Thinking.* Retrieved 30 September 2021 Online (last access on january 5th 2023): www.ineteconomics.org/perspectives/blog/how-the-term-mainstream-economics-became-mainstream-a-speculation.

Clots-Figueras, Irma, and Paolo Masella. 2013. 'Education, Language and Identity'. *The Economic Journal* 123(570):F332–57. https://doi.org/10.1111/ecoj.12051.

Cronin, Bruce. 2016. 'Multiple and Mixed Methods Research for Economics'. Pp. 286–300 in *Handbook of Research Methods and Applications in Heterodox Economics*, edited by F. Lee and B. Cronin. Cheltenham: Edward Elgar.

Cruz-e-Silva, Victor, and Marco Cavalieri. 2021. 'A Coherentist Defense of Economics as an Interdisciplinary Social Science'. *Journal of Economic Issues* 55(3):820–36. https:// doi.org/10.1080/00213624.2021.1948278.

Davis, John B. 2006. 'Social Identity Strategies in Recent Economics'. *Journal of Economic Methodology* 13(3):371–90. https://doi.org/10.1080/13501780600908168.

Davis, John B. 2010. 'Neuroeconomics: Constructing Identity'. *Journal of Economic Behavior & Organization* 76(3):574–83. https://doi.org/10.1016/j.jebo.2010.08.011.

Davis, John B. 2011. *Individuals and Identity in Economics*. Cambridge: Cambridge University Press.

Deprez, Steff, Caroline Huyghe, and Claudia Van Gool Maldonado. 2012. *Using Sensemaker to Measure, Learn and Communicate about Smallholder Farmer Inclusion*. Leuven: Vredeseilanden/VECO.

Deruytter, Laura, and Sebastian Möller. 2020. 'Cultures of Debt Management Enter City Hall'. Pp. 400–10 in *The Routledge International Handbook of Financialization*, edited by P. Mader, D. Mertens, and N. van der Zwan. London; New York: Routledge.

Dorn, Franziska, Simone Maxand, and T. Kneib. 2021. 'The Dependence between Income Inequality and Carbon Emissions: A Distributional Copula Analysis'. *SSRN Electronic Journal*. https://doi.org/10.2139/ssrn.3800302.

Düppe, Till. 2009. 'The Phenomenology of Economics: Life-World, Formalism, and the Invisible Hand'. *Journal of the History of Economic Thought* 32(4):609–611.

Enste, Dominik H., Alexandra Haferkamp, and Detlef Fetchenhauer. 2009. 'Unterschiede Im Denken Zwischen Ökonomen Und Laien – Erklärungsansätze Zur Verbesserung Der Wirtschaftspolitischen Beratung'. *Perspektiven Der Wirtschaftspolitik* 10(1):60–78. https://doi.org/10.1111/j.1468-2516.2008.00294.x.

Fainshmidt, Stav, William Q. Judge, Ruth V. Aguilera, and Adam Smith. 2018. 'Varieties of Institutional Systems: A Contextual Taxonomy of Understudied Countries'. *Journal of World Business* 53(3):307–22. https://doi.org/10.1016/j.jwb.2016.05.003.

Finch, John H. 1997. '"Verstehen," Ideal Types, and Situational Analysis and the Problem of Free Will'. *Journal of Institutional and Theoretical Economics* 153(4):737–47. www.jstor.org/stable/40752029.

Finch, John H. 2002. 'The Role of Grounded Theory in Developing Economic Theory'. *Journal of Economic Methodology* 9(2):213–34. https://doi.org/10.1080/13501780210137119.

Fine, B. 2008. 'The Economics of Identity and the Identity of Economics?'. *Cambridge Journal of Economics* 33(2):175–91. https://doi.org/10.1093/cje/ben036.

Fleetwood, Steve. 2008. 'Structure, Institution, Agency, Habit, and Reflexive Deliberation'. *Journal of Institutional Economics* 4(2):183–203. https://doi.org/10.1017/S1744137408000957.

Flick, Uwe, ed. 2014. *The SAGE Handbook of Qualitative Data Analysis*. Los Angeles: SAGE.

Frey, Bruno S., and Stephan Meier. 2003. 'Are Political Economists Selfish and Indoctrinated? Evidence from a Natural Experiment'. *Economic Inquiry* 41(3):448–62. https://doi.org/10.1093/ei/cbg020.

Frey, Bruno S., and Stephan Meier. 2005. 'Selfish and Indoctrinated Economists?'. *European Journal of Law and Economics* 19(2):165–71. https://doi.org/10.1007/s10657-005-5425-8.

Frey, Bruno S., Werner W. Pommerehne, and Beat Gygi. 1993. 'Economics Indoctrination or Selection? Some Empirical Results'. *The Journal of Economic Education* 24(3):271–81.

Fricker, Miranda. 2007. *Epistemic Injustice: Power and the Ethics of Knowing*. Oxford; New York: Oxford University Press.

Frollová, Nikola, Marek Vranka, and Petr Houdek. 2021. 'A Qualitative Study of Perception of a Dishonesty Experiment'. *Journal of Economic Methodology* 28(3):1–17. https://doi.org/10.1080/1350178X.2021.1936598.

Gerrard, Bill. 1993. 'The Significance of Interpretation in Economics'. Pp. 51–63 in *Economics and Language*, edited by R. Backhouse. London; New York: Routledge.

Gibson, Katherine, and Kelly Dombroski, eds. 2020. *The Handbook of Diverse Economies*. Cheltenham: Edward Elgar.

Glaser, Barney G. 2008. *Doing Quantitative Grounded Theory*. Mill Valley: Sociology Press.

Glaser, Barney G., and Anselm L. Strauss. 1967. *The Discovery of Grounded Theory: Strategies for Qualitative Research*. New Brunswick: Aldine Transaction.

Graupe, Silja. 2007. *The Basho of Economics: An Intercultural Analysis of the Process of Economics*. Frankfurt a.M.: Ontos.

Graupe, Silja. 2016. 'Der erstarrte Blick. Eine erkenntnistheoretische Einführung der Standardlehrbücher der Volkswirtschaftslehre'. Pp. 18–26 in *Wirtschaft neu denken. Blinde Flecken in der Lehrbuchökonomie*, edited by T. van Treeck and J. Urban. Berlin: iRights Media.

Gregory, Jane, and Steve Miller. 2000. *Science in Public: Communication, Culture, and Credibility*. Cambridge: Basic Books.

Greiffenhagen, Christian, Michael Mair, and Wes Sharrock. 2011. 'From Methodology to Methodography: A Study of Qualitative and Quantitative Reasoning in Practice'. *Methodological Innovations Online* 6(3):93–107. https://doi.org/10.4256/mio.2011.009.

Hall, Peter A., and David W. Soskice, eds. 2001. *Varieties of Capitalism: The Institutional Foundations of Comparative Advantage*. Oxford: Oxford University Press.

Haucap, Justus, and Tobias Just. 2010. 'Not Guilty? Another Look at the Nature and Nurture of Economics Students'. *European Journal of Law and Economics* 29(2):239–54. https://doi.org/10.1007/s10657-009-9119-5.

Hecker, Susanne, Muki Haklay, Anne Bowser, Zen Makuch, Johannes Vogel, and Aletta Bonn, eds. 2018. *Citizen Science: Innovation in Open Science, Society and Policy*. London: UCL Press.

Hellmich, Simon Niklas. 2019. 'Are People Trained in Economics "Different," and If so, Why? A Literature Review'. *The American Economist* 64(2):246–68. https://doi.org/10.1177/0569434519829433.

Hodgson, Geoffrey M. 2003. 'The Hidden Persuaders: Institutions and Individuals in Economic Theory'. *Cambridge Journal of Economics* 27(2):159–75. https://doi.org/10.1093/cje/27.2.159.

Hodgson, Geoffrey M. 2004. *The Evolution of Institutional Economics: Agency, Structure, and Darwinism in American Institutionalism*. London; New York: Routledge.

Horst, Ulrich, Alan Kirman, and Miriam Teschl. 2007. 'Changing Identity: The Emergence of Social Groups'. *Institute for Advanced Study, School of Social Science Economics Working Papers* 78. Online (last access on march 28th 2023): https://www.ias.edu/sites/default/files/sss/papers/econpaper78.pdf

Huettel, S. A., and R. E. Kranton. 2012. 'Identity Economics and the Brain: Uncovering the Mechanisms of Social Conflict'. *Philosophical Transactions of the Royal Society B: Biological Sciences* 367(1589):680–91. https://doi.org/10.1098/rstb.2011.0264.

Husserl, Edmund. 1984. *The Crisis of European Sciences and Transcendental Phenomenology: An Introduction to Phenomenological Philosophy*. 6th pr. Evanston, IL: Northwestern University Press.

Iida, Yoshio, and Sobei H. Oda. 2011. 'Does Economics Education Make Bad Citizens? The Effect of Economics Education in Japan'. *Journal of Education for Business* 86(4):234–39. https://doi.org/10.1080/08832323.2010.511303.

Jackson, William A. 2009. *Economics, Culture and Social Theory.* Cheltenham: Edward Elgar.

Johnson, Samuel G. 2019. 'Toward a Cognitive Science of Markets: Economic Agents as Sense-Makers'. *Economics: The Open-Access, Open-Assessment E-Journal* 13(2019–49). https://doi.org/10.5018/economics-ejournal.ja.2019-49.

Kaiser, Jonas, Kasper Pedersen, and Alexander Koch. 2018. 'Do Economists Punish Less?'. *Games* 9(4):75. https://doi.org/10.3390/g9040075.

Kara, Helen. 2020. *Creative Research Methods: A Practical Guide.* Bristol: Bristol University Press.

Keske, Catherine M., Dana L. Hoag, Donald M. McLeod, Christopher T. Bastian, and Michael G. Lacy. 2011. 'Using Mixed Methods Research in Environmental Economics: The Case of Conservation Easements'. *International Journal of Mixed Methods in Applied Business and Policy Research* 1(1):16–28.

Klebaner, Samuel, and Matthieu Montalban. 2020. 'Cross-Fertilizations Between Institutional Economics and Economic Sociology: The Case of Régulation Theory and the Sociology of Fields'. *Review of Political Economy* 32(2):180–98. https://doi.org/10.1080/09538259.2019.1674484.

Klein, Olivier, Stéphane Doyen, Christophe Leys, Pedro A. Magalhães de Saldanha da Gama, Sarah Miller, Laurence Questienne, and Axel Cleeremans. 2012. 'Low Hopes, High Expectations: Expectancy Effects and the Replicability of Behavioral Experiments'. *Perspectives on Psychological Science* 7(6):572–84. https://doi.org/10.1177/1745691612463704.

Kroncke, Charles O. 1993. 'Are Economists Different? An Empirical Note'. *The Social Science Journal* 30(4):341–45. https://doi.org/10.1016/0362-3319(93)90013-L.

Kurrild-Klitgaard, Peter. 2001. 'On Rationality, Ideal Types and Economics: Alfred Schütz and the Austrian School'. *The Review of Austrian Economics* 14(2/3):119–43. https://doi.org/10.1023/A:1011199831428.

Lamla, Jörn. 2009. 'Konsumpraktiken in der virtuellen Alltagsökonomie'. Pp. 779–803 in *Qualitative Marktforschung,* edited by R. Buber and H. H. Holzmüller. Wiesbaden: Gabler.

Lavoie, Don, ed. 1991. *Economics and Hermeneutics.* London; New York: Routledge.

Lawson, Tony. 1987. 'The Relative/Absolute Nature of Knowledge and Economic Analysis'. *The Economic Journal* 97(388):951. https://doi.org/10.2307/2233082.

Lawson, Tony. 1997. *Economics and Reality.* London; New York: Routledge.

Lee, Frederic. 2005. 'Grounded Theory and Heterodox Economics'. *The Grounded Theory Review* 4(2):95–110.

Lee, Frederic. 2016. 'Critical Realism, Method of Grounded Theory, and Theory Construction'. Pp. 35–53 in *Handbook of Research Methods and Applications in Heterodox Economics,* edited by F. Lee and B. Cronin. Cheltenham: Edward Elgar.

Lee, Frederic, and Bruce Cronin. 2016. *Handbook of Research Methods and Applications in Heterodox Economics.* Cheltenham: Edward Elgar.

Lenger, Alexander. 2019. 'The Rejection of Qualitative Research Methods in Economics'. *Journal of Economic Issues* 53(4):946–65. https://doi.org/10.1080/00213624.2019.1657748.

Lenger, Alexander, and Martin Buchner. 2018. 'Was Denken (Zukünftige) Ökonom*innen? Befunde Aus Dem Feld Der Soziologie Ökonomischen Denkens

Und Ihre Konsequenzen Für Das Studium Der Wirtschaftswissenschaften'. *GWP –
Gesellschaft. Wirtschaft. Politik* 67(3):351–59. https://doi.org/10.3224/gwp.v67i3.07.

López-Pérez, Raúl, and Eli Spiegelman. 2019. 'Do Economists Lie More?'. Pp. 143–62
in *Dishonesty in Behavioral Economics*. London: Academic Press.

Lune, Howard, and Bruce L. Berg. 2017. *Qualitative Research Methods for the Social Sciences*. 9th ed. Harlow: Pearson.

Maasen, Sabine, and Oliver Lieven. 2006. 'Transdisciplinarity: A New Mode
of Governing Science?'. *Science and Public Policy* 33(6):399–410. https://doi.
org/10.3152/147154306781778803.

Mankiw, N. Gregory. 2021. *Principles of Economics*. 9th ed. Boston: Cengage Learning.

Marshall, Alfred. 1920. *Principles of Economics: An Introductory Volume*. 8th ed. London:
Macmillan Press Ltd.

Marwell, Gerald, and Ruth E. Ames. 1981. 'Economists Free Ride, Does Anyone Else?'. *Journal of Public Economics* 15(3):295–310. https://doi.org/10.1016/
0047-2727(81)90013-X.

Matthews, D. 2006. 'Epistemic Humility'. Pp. 105–37 in *Wisdom, Knowledge, and Management*, edited by J. P. van Gigch. New York: Springer.

McCloskey, Deirdre N. 2000. *How to Be Human – Though an Economist*. Ann Arbor:
University of Michigan Press.

Mennicken, Andrea, and Wendy Nelson Espeland. 2019. 'What's New with Numbers?
Sociological Approaches to the Study of Quantification'. *Annual Review of Sociology*
45(1):223–45. https://doi.org/10.1146/annurev-soc-073117-041343.

Mertens, Donna M. 2009. *Transformative Research and Evaluation*. New York: Guilford Press.

Merton, Robert C. 1973. 'The Normative Structure of Science'. Pp. 267–78 in *The Sociology of Science: Theoretical and Empirical Investigations*. Chicago: University of Chicago Press.

Mirowski, Philip. 1987. 'The Philosophical Bases of Institutionalist Economics'. *Journal
of Economic Issues* 21(3):1001–38. https://doi.org/10.1080/00213624.1987.11504695.

Mügge, Daniel. 2020. 'Economic Statistics as Political Artefacts'. *Review of International
Political Economy*:1–22. https://doi.org/10.1080/09692290.2020.1828141.

Mulgan, Geoff. 2021. 'The Case for Exploratory Social Sciences'. *The New Institute Discussion Papers*. Online (last access on march 28th 2023): https://thenew.institute/en/
media/the-case-for-exploratory-social-sciences

Nagel, Thomas. 1986. *The View from Nowhere*. 1st ed. New York: Oxford University Press.

Noddings, Nel. 2002. *Starting at Home: Caring and Social Policy*. Berkeley: University of
California Press.

Nowell, Clifford, and Doug Laufer. 1997. 'Undergraduate Student Cheating in the Fields
of Business and Economics'. *The Journal of Economic Education* 28(1):3–12. https://doi.
org/10.1080/00220489709595901.

O'Roark, J. Brian. 2012. 'Does Economic Education Make a Difference in Congress?
How Economics Majors Vote on Trade'. *The Journal of Economic Education* 43(4):423–
39. https://doi.org/10.1080/00220485.2012.714319.

Ostrom, Elinor. 2005. *Understanding Institutional Diversity*. Princeton: Princeton University Press.

Paxton, Julia. 2019. 'Economics Training and Hyperbolic Discounting: Training versus
Selection Effects'. *Applied Economics* 51(55):5891–99. https://doi.org/10.1080/0003
6846.2019.1631439.

Pickbourn, Lynda, and Smita Ramnarain. 2016. 'Separate or Symbiotic? Quantitative and Qualitative Methods in (Heterodox) Economics Research'. Pp. 73–91 in

Handbook of Research Methods and Applications in Heterodox Economics, edited by F. Lee and B. Cronin. Cheltenham: Edward Elgar.

Pratten, Stephen. 2013. 'Critical Realism and the Process Account of Emergence: Critical Realism and the Process Account of Emergence'. *Journal for the Theory of Social Behaviour* 43(3):251–79. https://doi.org/10.1111/jtsb.12017.

Przyborski, Aglaja, and Monika Wohlrab-Sahr. 2021. *Qualitative Sozialforschung: ein Arbeitsbuch*. 5th ed. München: Oldenbourg.

Reichertz, Jo. 1993. 'Abduktives Schlußfolgern Und Typen(Re)Konstruktion'. Pp. 258–82 in *'Wirklichkeit' im Deutungsprozeß: Verstehen und Methoden in den Kultur- und Sozialwissenschaften*, edited by T. Jung and S. Müller-Doohm. Frankfurt a.M.: Suhrkamp.

Rickman, Hans Peter. 1976. 'Introduction'. Pp. 1–32 in *Dilthey: Selected Writings*. Cambridge: Cambridge University Press.

Robinson, Joan. 2021. *Economic Philosophy*. London; New York: Routledge.

Rosser, John Barkley, and Marina V. Rosser. 2004. *Comparative Economics in a Transforming World Economy*. 2nd ed. Cambridge, MA: MIT Press.

Rubinstein, Ariel. 2006. 'A Sceptic's Comment on the Study of Economics★'. *The Economic Journal* 116(510):C1–9. https://doi.org/10.1111/j.1468-0297.2006.01071.x.

Schefold, Bertram. 2004. 'Edgar Salin and His Concept of "Anschauliche Theorie" ("Intuitive Theory") During the Interwar Period'. *Annals of the Society for the History of Economic Thought* 46(46):1–16. https://doi.org/10.11498/jshet1963.46.1.

Schlaudt, Oliver. 2022. *Philosophy of Economics: A Heterodox Introduction*. Abingdon, Oxon ; New York, NY: Routledge.

Schlüter, Achim. 2010. 'Institutional Change and Qualitative Research: Methodological Considerations for Institutional Economic Empirical Research'. *Journal of Interdisciplinary Economics* 22(4):391–406. https://doi.org/10.1177/02601079X10002200405.

Schütz, Alfred. 1962. 'Common-Sense and Scientific Interpretation of Human Action'. Pp. 3–47 in *The Problem of Social Reality, Collected Papers*, edited by M. Natanson. Dordrecht: Springer Netherlands.

Schütz, Alfred. 1971. *Gesammelte Aufsätze I: Das Problem der sozialen Wirklichkeit*. The Hague: Martinus Nijhoff.

Selten, Reinhard, and Axel Ockenfels. 1998. 'An Experimental Solidarity Game'. *Journal of Economic Behavior & Organization* 34(4):517–39. https://doi.org/10.1016/S0167-2681(97)00107-8.

Shackle, G. L. S. 1992. *Epistemics & Economics: A Critique of Economic Doctrines*. New Brunswick: Transaction Publishers.

Snowden, Dave. 2005. 'Stories from the Frontier'. *E:CO* 7(3–4):155–65.

Srinivas, Smita. 2020. 'Institutional Variety and the Future of Economics'. *Review of Evolutionary Political Economy* 1(1):13–35. https://doi.org/10.1007/s43253-020-00010-7.

Starr, Martha A. 2014. 'Qualitative and Mixed-Methods Research in Economics: Surprising Growth, Promising Future'. *Journal of Economic Surveys* 28(2):238–64. https://doi.org/10.1111/joes.12004.

Storper, Michael, and Robert Salais. 1997. *Worlds of Production: The Action Frameworks of the Economy*. Cambridge, MA: Harvard University Press.

Stumpf, Lukas, Josef-Peter Schöggl, and Rupert J. Baumgartner. 2021. 'Climbing up the Circularity Ladder? – A Mixed-Methods Analysis of Circular Economy in Business Practice'. *Journal of Cleaner Production* 316:128–58. https://doi.org/10.1016/j.jclepro.2021.128158.

Sum, Ngai-Ling, and Bob Jessop. 2013. *Towards a Cultural Political Economy: Putting Culture in Its Place in Political Economy*. Cheltenham: Edward Elgar.

Svetlova, Ekaterina. 2008. *Sinnstiftung in der Ökonomik: wirtschaftliches Handeln aus sozial-philosophischer Sicht*. Bielefeld: transcript.

Swedberg, Richard, Gary S. Becker, James S. Coleman, George A. Akerlof, Harrison C. White, Mark Granovetter, Oliver E. Williamson, Kenneth J. Arrow, Albert O. Hirschman, Mancur Olson, Thomas C. Schelling, Neil J. Smelser, Daniel Bell, Jon Elster, Amartya Sen, Robert M. Solow, Arthur L. Stincbcombe, and Aage B. Sørensen. 2020. *Economics and Sociology: Redefining Their Boundaries: Conversations with Economists and Sociologists*. Princeton: Princeton University Press.

Tuckett, David. 2012. 'Financial Markets Are Markets in Stories: Some Possible Advantages of Using Interviews to Supplement Existing Economic Data Sources'. *Journal of Economic Dynamics and Control* 36(8):1077–87. https://doi.org/10.1016/j.jedc.2012.03.013.

Unger, Roberto Mangabeira. 1978. 'Illusions of Necessity in the Economic Order'. *The American Economic Review* 68(2):369–73.

Unger, Roberto Mangabeira. 1987. *False Necessity: Anti-Necessitarian Social Theory in the Service of Radical Democracy*. Cambridge: Cambridge University Press.

Unger, Roberto Mangabeira. 2007. *The Self Awakened: Pragmatism Unbound*. Cambridge, MA: Harvard University Press.

Unger, Roberto Mangabeira, and Lee Smolin. 2015. *The Singular Universe and the Reality of Time: A Proposal in Natural Philosophy*. Cambridge: Cambridge University Press.

Vallet, Guillaume, and Steven Pressman. 2020. 'Economics and Sociology: An Introduction'. *Review of Political Economy* 32(2):141–48. https://doi.org/10.1080/09538259.2020.1803599.

Van der Merwe, Susara E., Reinette Biggs, Rika Preiser, Charmaine Cunningham, David J. Snowden, Karen O'Brien, Marcus Jenal, Marietjie Vosloo, Sonja Blignaut, and Zhen Goh. 2019. 'Making Sense of Complexity: Using SenseMaker as a Research Tool'. *Systems* 7(2):1–19. https://doi.org/10.3390/systems7020025.

Veblen, Thorstein. 1898. 'Why Is Economics Not an Evolutionary Science?'. *The Quarterly Journal of Economics* 12(4):373–97. https://doi.org/10.2307/1882952.

Wang, Long, Deepak Malhotra, and J. Keith Murnighan. 2011. 'Economics Education and Greed'. *Academy of Management Learning & Education* 10(4):643–60. https://doi.org/10.5465/amle.2009.0185.

Wisman, Jon D. 1979. 'Toward a Humanist Reconstruction of Economic Science'. *Journal of Economic Issues* 13(1):19–48. https://doi.org/10.1080/00213624.1979.11503609.

Yezer, Anthony M., Robert S. Goldfarb, and Paul J. Poppen. 1996. 'Does Studying Economics Discourage Cooperation? Watch What We Do, Not What We Say or How We Play'. *Journal of Economic Perspectives* 10(1):177–86. https://doi.org/10.1257/jep.10.1.177.

7 Conclusion

Now that a way to re-think the economy and a respective economics has been presented, one way to proceed could be the exemplification of the account given. In fact, this was done in a preceding German-language publication with regard to the self-signification processes occurring in economics itself (Bäuerle 2022). With regard to 'typical economic' phenomena, as the numerous examples mentioned in Chapter 6 indicate, Grounded Economics will not have to start from scratch. Instead, it might be understood as a convergent momentum of interdisciplinary impulses co-existing next to each other. A subsequent publication will dwell on a plurality of examples in methodical and theoretical terms that could be reframed as precursors of a Grounded Economics in the specific sense outlined here: a form of economic research genuinely interested to learn how people actually 'do the economy' out there. So, instead of zooming in for the remainder of this book, we will zoom out to gain perspective for the (possible) meaning of the innovations provided in and for the time it was written.

Husserl's diagnosis of crisis-laden modern science stemmed from its loss of the lifeworld as the ultimate point of reference, as its only viable source of meaningfulness (Hua VI, §2). Almost a century later, a very similar crisis is catching up with humanity in its entirety. Public awareness is growing about mankind's devastating effect on its single lifeworld. Humanity is losing the lifeworld through self-inflicted actions. To be more precise: it is losing *certain qualities* of the lifeworld as they were given to humanity up to this point. It is losing *livelihoods*. The lifeworld in Husserl's sense, as primordial 'stage', will ever be there for the living, however distorted it might become. The processes of a loss of livelihoods, its successive destruction, have reached such a degree on the threshold to the second quarter of the 21st century that the fragility of the intangible 'stage' is becoming apparent. "Life is living in constant world-certainty" (Hua VI, 145). Would we agree today? The fragility of life on earth not only applies to the genuinely ecological dimensions of the lifeworld but also to its social dimensions, as manifested in phenomena of extreme social inequality and existential poverty (cf. Alvaredo et al. 2017; Institute for Policy Studies 2021). In the Anthropocene, the green surface in the background is

DOI: 10.4324/9781003371687-7

shaking due to the established red rhombuses in the foreground. In more modern terms: at the latest point in the Anthropocene, every ecological question boils down to a social one. The destruction of certain social and ecological aspects of the lifeworld is of equal origin. It runs through institutionalised social practices and relationships that we reproduce every day and on a global scale. Transforming these relationships is becoming an existential issue. The scientific bodies that global society has given itself to assess its situation are unambiguous in their diagnosis (cf. IPCC 2018:3, 2015:2.2–2.4; IPBES and IPCC 2021:6 ff.; United Nations and Department of Economic and Social Affairs 2020): The causes of the lifeworld's shaking lie in the globally normalised practices of 'doing the economy'. The performativity of humanity, and most aggressively, of its economic institutions, is not merely affecting and increasing the number of life's *aspects* but actually life's *foundations*. Hence the call to alter these habitual practices of 'the economy' (the 'what?' of transformation) in order to preserve the basis of life for as many living beings as possible (a possible 'why?' of transformation). The role played by the different forms of practice on the vertical axis (the 'how?' of transformation) and from where the impulse for change is initiated and carried through on the horizontal axis (the 'who?' of transformation) – these intricacies are assessed in wide and conflicting ranges. Wide consensus exists, however, that the ongoing loss of livelihoods can only be mitigated if the knowledge already obtained in reflexive practices and the potentialities inherent in all forms of practice are drastically translated into new *habitual* practices of 'doing the economy'. A progressing transformation of Planet Earth must be addressed by a transformation of the economic institutions around the world.

Now that 'the economy' has grown into humanity's crucial 'matter of concern' (Latour), what could the role of a Grounded Economics be? Chapter 6 argued for an *epistemic* re-relating to tangible phenomena against the backdrop of doing *epistemic* justice to them. As the recent history of economics shows, the discipline is deeply embedded in the wider social arena. It is always also part of the *political* designing of society. Here, too, a re-relating of the discipline appears to be necessary. Instead of retreating from the public sphere in order to contain an imperialist tradition, another path shall be considered here for Grounded Economists. As concerned with down-to-earth economic matters *ex professio*, they could form a crucial part of a political process in a specific notion:

Each object gathers around itself a different assembly of relevant parties. Each object triggers new occasions to passionately differ and dispute. Each object may also offer new ways of achieving closure without having to agree on much else. In other words, objects – taken as so many issues – bind all of us in ways that map out a public space profoundly different from what is usually recognized under the label of 'the political'. . . . If the Ding designates both those who assemble because they are concerned as well as what causes their concerns and divisions, it should become the center of our attention: Back to Things!

(Latour 2005:15, 23)

Following Latour, Grounded Economists, via a reorientation towards tangible economic matters, inescapably form part of a public. Against the backdrop of the specific notion the public is starting to address with economic matters, it might be specified as the arena of economic transformation. Grounded Economists are not just distant observers of this arena but participating agents. To contribute to the issues of this public arena is becoming not just an add-on but an existential issue. Five possible contributions shall be identified here. Grounded Economists can:

1 Keep alive the public deliberations about the matter of concern – 'the economy' as such. It can provoke the discussion about what to signify as 'the economy', remind the general public about the fundamental openness of this process and its temporary outcomes and point to blind spots and/or proactive attempts of imaginative enclosures. Instead of propagating their own stakes, they could help build and maintain critical, peaceful and fact-based discussions by the stakeholders in far or close reaching economic transformations. In doing so, it can help to (re)connect agents and things of a future-fit economy ever in the making. Since this activity implies a shift in power balances, it will cause ongoing disruptions and conflicts. A decisive question then becomes: "How can we reshape without fighting or fight without hurting?" (Unger 2007:164).

2 Gather knowledge about the economic status quo by means of 'down-to-earth' research in specific arenas of economic transformation. As laid out in Chapter 6, this implies looking beyond the usual figures and indicators that 'depict' the economy as of today in order to provide a grounded picture of where things actually stand for all stakeholders involved. Methodically speaking, this would mean a drastic increase in reconstructive, ethnographic and participatory research approaches when compared to the standard economic toolbox.

3 Point to potentialities of economic transformation; for instance, along the systematics as given in this book's framework (Chapters 2–4) and the processual implication involved from moving from A to B. This would imply a radical expansion of the understanding of human agency in economic matters: people driven by imagination and reflection rather than by memory or programming. It would also imply the stark affirmation of alterity and plurality as crucial drivers of economic development.

4 Provide proper educational programmes, aiming to foster those capabilities needed in order to understand (Point 2) and transform (Point 3) the economy. Crucially, these capacities will not be guided by the motivations/ends of Grounded Economists but by the people engaged. For both in epistemic

and practical terms, it must remain in their freedom to direct the course of action taken.

5 Engage in co-creative transformation processes themselves, as given in living or design labs, for instance. Instead of controlling social interactions, scholars join a creative process that aims at the mutual reconfiguration of sociality as such. This does not mean to even out different backgrounds or capabilities, but rather, connect them in a design process built around a shared goal (for instance, how to transform − specific aspects of − 'the economy' in our city?).

These are suggestions, formulated with the aim to provoke discussions rather than end them. With Husserl, they aim at a renewed meaningfulness of economic science. But more importantly, they aim at a meaningful economy in and for the lifeworld of our times. This meaningfulness is not a distant utopia to be reached but a never-ending task of collective renewal in and of economic terms. And it can only be maintained if people are granted agency; if they are given a chance to outlive their potentials, to follow their purpose. The good news is: no one has to wait for a renewed economics or economic education in order to trigger such a process. It can be initiated here and now, even if not necessarily in the institutional places actually intended for it. The ultimate contextualisation of 'the economy' does not lie in economics − but in the lifeworld. To fathom the meaning of a future-fit economy performatively and to let it draw larger circles together with others, this can be done anytime, anywhere, under the condition of a minimum of existential security (of livelihoods) and mutual trust. Let us use it, we who enjoy this security, to maintain or create it for as many as possible − before we lose it in adversity. In other words: let us transform by design!

References

Alvaredo, Facundo, Lucas Chancel, Thomas Piketty, Emmanuel Saez, and Gabriel Zucman. 2017. *World Inequality Report 2018*. World Inequality Lab.
Bäuerle, Lukas. 2022. *Ökonomie − Praxis − Subjektivierung. Eine Praxeologische Institutionenforschung Am Beispiel Ökonomischer Hochschulbildung*. Bielefeld: transcript.
Institute for Policy Studies. 2021. 'Facts'. *Inequality.Org*. Retrieved 18 June 2021 Online (last access on january 5th 2023): https://inequality.org/facts/.
IPBES and IPCC. 2021. 'Biodiversity and Climate Change'. Online (last access on march 28th 2023): https://www.ipbes.net/sites/default/files/2021-06/20210609_scientific_outcome.pdf
IPCC. 2015. 'Climate Change 2014: Synthesis Report'. Online (last access on march 28th 2023): https://www.ipcc.ch/report/ar5/syr/
IPCC. 2018. 'Global Warming of 1.5°C. An IPCC Special Report on the Impacts of Global Warming of 1.5°C above Pre-Industrial Levels and Related Global Greenhouse Gas Emission Pathways, in the Context of Strengthening the Global Response to the Threat of Climate Change, Sustainable Development, and Efforts to Eradicate Poverty'. Online (last access on march 28th 2023): https://www.ipcc.ch/site/assets/uploads/sites/2/2019/06/

SR15_Full_Report_Low_Res.pdf#%5B%7B%22num%22%3A589%2C%22gen%22%3A0%7D%2C%7B%22name%22%3A%22FitH%22%7D%2C792%5D

Latour, Bruno. 2005. 'From Realpolitik to Dingpolitik or How to Make Things Public'. Pp. 14–42 in *Making Things Public: Atmospheres of Democracy*, edited by B. Latour and P. Weibel. Cambridge, MA: MIT Press.

Unger, Roberto Mangabeira. 2007. *The Self Awakened: Pragmatism Unbound*. Cambridge, MA: Harvard University Press.

United Nations and Department of Economic and Social Affairs. 2020. *World Social Report 2020: Inequality in a Rapidly Changing World*. New York: United Nations Publishing.

Index

agency 4–5, 20, 23–7, 33–6, 55, 102–3, 115n3, 116
artefacts 25, 43, 78, 94

behavioural economics 2, 19, 57, 70n5, 86–7, 104n5, 104n7
body 32–4, 46nn11–13

capabilities 2, 6n2, 116
co-creation 4, 41, 116
commons 2

ecological economics 2
economic methodology 6, 17–27, 33, 44n1, 44n5, 55–6, 65, 70n3, 85–104
economic sociology 2, 78
economisation 3
the economy 1–6, 14–15, 76–82, 116
embeddednes 4, 94
epistemic justice 92–5, 104n10, 114
experiences 11–13, 34–5, 95–6, 104n10
experiments 6n2, 19, 87–8, 103n4, 104n5

feminist economics 2, 79
freedom 6n2, 19–21, 35–8, 46n16, 116

grounded theory 91, 100

habits 28–30, 56–61, 65–70, 70n2, 70n4, 70n5, 71n6, 86, 94, 114
horizontal gap 31, 35

imagination 3–4, 42, 56, 63–6
individuality 12, 17–27, 44n3, 66, 87, 93

institutional agency 23–7, 31–3, 55
institutionalism 5, 24–31, 44n1, 45n8, 60, 69, 101
institutional transformation 30–43, 58–9
institutions 2, 14, 23–46, 55, 59–61, 64–9, 78–82, 91, 101, 114
interdisciplinarity 5, 102, 113

lifeworld 11–12, 113–14

The Market Mechanism 1–2, 65, 70n3, 82
materiality 13, 25, 43, 69
methodological holism 21–3
methodological individualism 17–21

neoliberalism 1, 3, 82
normativity 80, 90–3, 98, 115–16

ontologisation 18, 24, 100

performativity of economics 3–4, 68
phenomenology 5, 11–13, 33, 46n11, 63–5, 70n1, 94–5, 100
pluralism 7n2, 82, 97, 99, 102, 115
potentiality 5, 31–43, 59, 65
pragmatism 5, 44n1
praxeology 25, 38, 70n3, 80, 98
praxis 13, 25, 36, 44n6, 53–72, 91, 115
primordial gap 11–15, 90
process philosophy 44n5

reflection 13, 25, 37, 41, 44n6, 53–72, 91, 115
relationality 18–19, 24, 44n5, 99

scientific freedom 93
self-transformation 30–43, 45n9, 63
sense-making 12–15, 24–5, 35, 44n5,
    53–8, 77–8, 85–6, 96
social imaginaries 3, 12–15, 25, 31,
    35–40, 65, 70n4, 77
social structures 21–31, 38, 40–43,
    44n6, 101
Social Studies of Economi cs 1, 71n8
socioeconomics 2, 5, 78, 101

standard economics 2, 30, 71n8, 72n12,
    77–80, 85–90, 95
subjectivation 28–30, 45n8, 45n9, 69
sustainability 1

transformation 1, 3–5, 23–44, 46n18,
    58–9, 63, 114–16

vertical gap 53–7, 63

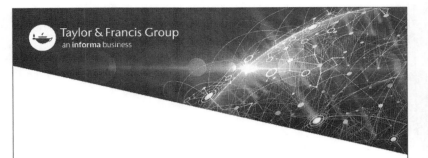

Printed in the United States
by Baker & Taylor Publisher Services